RISK-BASED POLICING

RISK-BASED POLICING

*Evidence-Based Crime Prevention with
Big Data and Spatial Analytics*

Leslie W. Kennedy
Joel M. Caplan
Eric L. Piza

UNIVERSITY OF CALIFORNIA PRESS

University of California Press, one of the most distinguished university presses in the United States, enriches lives around the world by advancing scholarship in the ities, social sciences, and natural sciences. Its activities are supported by the UC Press Foundation and by philanthropic contributions from individuals and institutions. For more information, visit www.ucpress.edu.

University of California Press
Oakland, California

© 2018 by The Regents of the University of California

Library of Congress Cataloging-in-Publication Data

Names: Kennedy, Leslie W., author. | Caplan, Joel M., 1980- author. | Piza, Eric L., 1981- author.
Title: Risk-based policing : evidence-based crime prevention with big data and spatial analytics / Leslie W. Kennedy, Joel M. Caplan, Eric L. Piza.
Description: Oakland, California : University of California Press, [2018] | Includes bibliographical references and index. |
Identifiers: LCCN 2018010269 (print) | LCCN 2018015036 (ebook) | ISBN 9780520968349 (ebook) | ISBN 9780520295636 (pbk. : alk. paper)
Subjects: LCSH: Crime prevention--Case studies. | Crime analysis--Data processing.
Classification: LCC HV7432 (ebook) | LCC HV7432 .K46 2018 (print) | DDC 363.2/3028557—dc23
LC record available at https://lccn.loc.gov/2018010269

27 26 25 24 23 22 21 20 19 18
10 9 8 7 6 5 4 3 2 1

CONTENTS

Preface · ix
Acknowledgments · xi

PART 1: THE BASIC PRINCIPLES OF RISK-BASED POLICING

1. Introduction to Risk and Big Data · 5
   Introduction to Risk-Based Policing in Crime Prevention · 5
   The Importance of Risk · 6
   Big Data · 8
   Risk-Based Policing · 8
   Conclusion · 9

2. The Evolution of Modern Policing · 11
   Introduction · 11
   Police Reform and Professionalization · 13
   From Professionalism to Problem-Solving · 16
   The Importance of Places and Data Analysis in Contemporary Policing · 18
   Conclusion · 21

3. Policing in the New Era of Public Safety and Law Enforcement · 23
   Focus on Places with Risk Terrain Modeling · 23
   The Central Tenets of Risk-Based Policing · 27

    Develop Spatial Risk Narratives · 27
    Solicit and Value Input from Multiple Stakeholders · 28
    Make Data-Driven Decisions · 30
    Balance Strategies for Crime Risk Reduction · 31
    Conclusion · 32

4. Risk-Based Policing and ACTION · 35
    Introduction · 35
    Risk Governance and the Police Leader · 36
    ACTION Meetings · 36
    A Detailed Breakdown of the ACTION Agenda · 39
    The Uncertainty in Risk Governance · 43
    Conclusion · 46

PART 2: METHODS AND CASE STUDIES OF RISK-BASED POLICING

5. The Theory of Risky Places · 53
    Introduction · 53
    Theories Relevant to Risk-Based Policing · 54
    Conclusion · 62

6. High-Risk Target Areas and Priority Places · 63
    Introduction · 63
    Studying Exposure and Vulnerability to Crime · 64
    Brooklyn as a Case Study · 65
    Conclusion · 70

7. The Role of Police in Risk-Based Policing: Case Studies of Colorado Springs, Glendale, Newark, and Kansas City · 71
    Introduction · 71
    Risk Assessment Methodology · 72
    Findings · 76
    Connecting Risk Assessments to Intervention · 98
    Conclusion · 100

8. Facilitators and Impediments to Designing, Implementing, and Evaluating Risk-Based Policing Strategies: Insights from Completed Researcher–Practitioner Partnerships · 102
    Introduction · 102
    Researcher–Practitioner Partnerships · 103
    Planned Change and Program Implementation · 104
    Risk-Based Policing Partnerships · 106
    Findings · 107
    Conclusion · 115

9. The Roles of Multiple Stakeholders in Risk-Based Policing:
   Case Studies of Jersey City and Atlantic City · 118
   Introduction · 118
   ACTION Meetings in Jersey City · 119
   Risk-Based Policing in Atlantic City · 120
   Conclusion · 124

10. People Make Risk-Based Policing and Data Actionable · 126
    Valuing Data: Lessons Learned · 126
    Beyond Training and into Active Problem Solving · 128
    Conclusion · 131

    Epilogue · 133
    References · 137
    Index · 149

PREFACE

Focusing on crime problems in terms of risk is not a new idea and has been discussed by various police researchers (e.g., Kennedy and Van Brunschot 2009; Gundhus 2005; Ericson and Haggerty 1997; Maguire 2000). Our experiences with risk-based policing were catalyzed by a meeting held at Michigan State University in 2009, sponsored by Ed McGarrell, where we discussed the broad implications of a risk-based approach to law enforcement. Since then, our attention has been focused on developing analytical tools and methods to provide evidence-based support for risk-based policing. In this book, we demonstrate how risk terrain modeling, which we discussed extensively in *Risk Terrain Modeling: Crime Prediction and Risk Reduction* (Caplan and Kennedy, 2016), can be extended beyond providing diagnoses of environmental attractors of criminal behavior and forecasts of crime settings to offer a more comprehensive view of prevention and deterrence. This is managed through an enterprise that focuses a police agency's abilities around risk governance in order to create efficient, effective, and sustainable responses to the crime and public safety challenges they face.

This book has two parts. We begin in part 1 with an overview of the principles of risk assessment and its relevance to crime analysis. We then provide an overview of past police practices and the relevance of risk-based policing to modern law enforcement agencies. Part 2 begins with a synopsis of the theoretical contexts in which these risk-based policing applications occur. We then present findings from a series of case studies that we have partnered on with agencies using risk terrain modeling for risk-based policing under different settings and conditions. We explore the methods, analytical techniques, and intervention strategies that were adopted and have become best practices in police departments around the country as a way of demonstrating the steps that can be taken to implement and validate the risk-based approach to policing.

ACKNOWLEDGMENTS

We would like to thank all of our colleagues, students, and agency partners who have worked with us to make the philosophy and practice of risk-based policing accessible, effective, and evidence-based. And thanks to the International Association of Crime Analysts and the American Society of Evidence-Based Policing for providing platforms that enabled us to incrementally share our work products with their membership and to receive constructive, grounded feedback. A very special thank you to Alejandro Giménez-Santana and Grant Drawve for helping us share, implement, and test risk-based policing around the world, and for training new generations of public safety leaders. We have been fortunate to benefit from the collective wisdom and talents of all of these people, and we are proud to share with the readers of this book the insightful products of our collaborations. Our work has been enthusiastically supported by Rutgers University and its School of Criminal Justice, the Rutgers Center on Public Security, and John Jay College of Criminal Justice, for which we are very grateful. We are also very appreciative of the financial support we have repeatedly received from the National Institute of Justice and the Bureau of Justice Assistance. We thank the entire team at the University of California Press, including the reviewers, who have been enthusiastic about this project and expended the effort and resources to successfully complete this book. In particular, we are grateful for the continued support and encouragement from our editor, Maura Roessner.

Les Kennedy, as always, would like to acknowledge the ongoing support and encouragement of his family members, Ilona, Alexis, Andrea, Stu, Espen, Helga, and my late father-in-law Alex. They have always shown an interest in my work and provide daily support for me as I continue to enjoy the interesting challenges of my ever-changing career. I would also like to give a special thanks to Joel, who continues to be an inspiration to me in our joint pursuit of innovative ideas. I am lucky to count him as a friend and colleague. I am fortunate, as well, to have found a friend in Eric, whose experience in policing has kept us grounded in our analysis and helped us produce relevant and actionable research. I am grateful that we have all had this time to work together and I anticipate many more collaborations in the future.

Joel Caplan would like to acknowledge the loving support of his family members, Oranit, Oriellah, and Shailee, and his parents Ron and Jackie. They allow me to pursue my professional goals while also enjoying the journey of life. Thank you for your encouragement and for being so amazing in so many ways. I would also like to thank Les and Eric. I am truly honored to call you my colleagues and friends. You are like family, and together we have realized that our scholarship can have so many rewards. Thank you for your honest opinions and confidence in our teamwork to change the world together.

Eric Piza would like to acknowledge the support of his wife, Diane. She has been extremely supportive, extremely helpful, and extremely caring throughout my career; I would not have accomplished much without her unwavering support. I am also thankful to my parents, Diosa and Hector, for always encouraging me to pursue my passions and supporting my career endeavors. Lastly, I am grateful to Les and Joel for being great mentors, collaborators, and friends over the years. From my time as a doctoral student to my current position as Associate Professor at John Jay, I have greatly benefitted from having Les and Joel as colleagues.

PART I

THE BASIC PRINCIPLES OF RISK-BASED POLICING

Risk-based policing is the mindset and operational practice of reducing and managing crime risks to prevent crime, with an emphasis on evidence-based decision-making, problem-solving, forecasting, transparency, efficient utilization of resources, and sustainability. There is a long history of innovations in policing, where research and planning have combined to produce successful interventions. A major outcome of these initiatives has been the realization that targeting police resources at risky places, based on smart uses of data and strong analytical work, can draw down the worst effects of disorder and can be effective in reducing and preventing crime. Considering how spatial risks affect all parts of the crime prevention enterprise for wide arrays of stakeholders makes efforts to deliver various services more effective.

1

INTRODUCTION TO RISK AND BIG DATA

> **KEY POINTS**
>
> - Risk-based policing focuses primarily on places and not people.
> - Risk analysis provides evidence-based support for risk narratives about how factors combine to increase the probability of crime occurrence.
> - Risk reduction strategies include specific information about where to go and also what to do when you get there.
> - Risk-based policing encourages community engagement and multi-stakeholder participation in crime prevention through risk reduction activities.

INTRODUCTION TO RISK-BASED POLICING IN CRIME PREVENTION

In discussing how crime prevention tactics have evolved, Bratton and Kelling (2012) admit that police too often focus on arresting their way out of crime problems. Still, they advocate that there needs to be a strategy for policing that is problem-oriented, properly resourced in terms of personnel, and targeted at the locations that need the most attention. Bratton and Kelling observe, correctly we believe, that police agencies have become very sophisticated in their problem-orientations, even leading other municipal agencies in their ways and means. This trend has been tied to the increased training and openness to higher education of police leadership, coupled with commensurate enabling sources of funding (often federal grants), making them receptive to new ideas and better planning. In this context, there is an openness (among at least some police agencies) to experiment and to expand on their missions. This has happened even when they have been confronting severely challenging expectations brought on by major divestments in urban areas after the global financial collapse of the early twenty-first century and discontent with the effects of policing practices on various community populations and constituents. We frame these problems in this book to propose risk-based policing as an effective and sustainable approach to a new policing frontier and social climate, based on evidence and insights from research, policy, and practice.

Risk-based policing considers more than the mere possibility that crime will occur, which has been a long-standing focus of criminology, crime prevention, and policing studies. Risk-based policing advocates addressing the contextual reasons for crime emergence and persistence at particular places. It does not rely on an actuarial count of the numbers of offenders and victims, or the potential that the one will inevitably prey on the other. It seeks to avoid a simplistic view of crime incident clustering that ignores the factors that repeatedly enable these behaviors at certain locations. It considers more than a focus on individual personal characteristics and looks at places that attract or repel criminal behaviors based on certain qualities. These qualities can be identified, operationalized, and compiled to determine their influence on criminal outcomes. Assessment of spatial influences of environmental conditions is not arbitrary, though. It is set in risk terrain models, where vulnerability to crime is diagnosed and charted based on pattern analysis, past experiences, and comparisons to other similar places. Risk provides the metric to be standardized, scaled to different levels of investigation, and contrasted over place and time.

THE IMPORTANCE OF RISK

Risk is a common metric, calculated by everyone who enters a particular landscape. We develop an understanding of how environments can protect or threaten us through visual cues, reputations, and perceptions that form fears, feelings of safety, or insecurity. Environments exhibit identifiable patterns. People size up what a location looks like and then judge it against their memories and assumptions about the causal links between certain environmental features and the likelihood that these will support criminal activity. Obviously, based on experience or knowledge of an area, these perceptions will vary, and may oftentimes be inaccurate. But even initial perceptions matter. Experiences, knowledge, and perceptions will also be different among various stakeholders depending on the roles that they play in these environments. Police see places they patrol through a different lens of risk than do inhabitants, tourists or passers-through. These risk assessments are important in shaping the expectations that each stakeholder forms in interacting with people at various places across the landscape.

Through advances in technology and better data we have been able to articulate the spatial influences that help form these risk perceptions. We have better evidence about how environments link to human behavior. It is this information that risk-based policing embraces to manage resources to mitigate these risks to prevent crime and enhance public safety. Risk terrain modeling (RTM) is an analytical engine for this problem-solving enterprise. It is embedded in a larger ecosystem in which decisions are made about the best ways to deliver services while reducing risks to police personnel and members of the community being served. With RTM, risk-based policing accounts for the insights that police officers and others who live and work in these communities bring to the table. These stakeholders, when encouraged to think in terms of risk governance, identify what (from their experiences) impacts on the quality of life in communities and leads to conditions that are ripe for crime. Their testimonials form an important set of data for law enforcement to aid risk governance and shape the results of RTM into multilateral plans for action.

Efforts by police agencies to reach out to community leaders and other stakeholders have benefited police by improving their relationships with these groups, particularly as they demand more accountability and transparency. But it is important that the information gleaned from these interactions consists of more than just complaints. Community engagement can be an integral part of the mechanism for police to share the burden of public safety with other stakeholders and to implement risk reduction programs in ways that meet everyone's expectations. When community members realize their role in crime prevention, they become partners to help solve existing crime problems and to identify and address emerging public safety threats. This keeps police officers safer, too.

Important in all of this, as well, is the understanding of what offenders use as indicators of their successful criminal behavior. Many criminals continue to operate in locations where conditions support their illegal activities, such as drug markets, or facilities that can attract illicit behavior, such as bars or convenience stores. Divestment in some cities, compounded by major economic failures, such as the housing foreclosure crisis, have changed the social relevancy of landscape features in many areas and made them high-risk for illegal outcomes. One advance in policing within the last few decades is an operational response to the fact that crimes cluster around other crimes over time, a phenomenon termed hot spots and a practice of hot spots policing. The advancement that underlies risk-based policing derives from an emphasis on the fact that features of the landscape also concentrate and interact, which explains why crime emerges or persists where it does. Hot spots policing, by going to hot spots and making arrests, which consequently increases the intensity of the hot spot, is self-fulfilling. This is offset by a risk-based approach that reduces crime in a way that does not rely on repeated crime occurrences in order to make new deployment decisions. The risk perspective shifts the focus from problem orientation to risk mitigation by considering all aspects of the environment, not just the role of the offender or the cluster of known crime incidents. Focusing on mitigating risk to achieve crime drops means the features that once attracted illegal behavior become less likely to encourage crime, which results in less attractive behavior settings for criminal offending. Vulnerability to crime is reduced, so the crime reduction is more sustainable and long-term. But, further, because police can measure what contributed to these risky conditions in the first place, they have a better understanding of what works and what does not in responding to and deterring criminal behavior. As a consequence, prevention strategies can be transported to other similar locations within the same jurisdictions, and implemented there with expectations of repeated success. This takes part of the guesswork out of policing and provides more evidence-based validations of best practices.

BIG DATA

Views and opinions of "places" have changed as technology and data have improved. Municipalities now collect more detailed and accurate geocoded information, which permits police not only to describe criminogenic places, but also to better understand the relationships between features of the environment and criminal behaviors. In addition, we can visualize places through tools like Google Street View, which adds real context to places and allows us to search them quickly and easily for cues about illegal behaviors that might be enabled or emerging. We can overlay on these places information about people who use them and how they inhabit them at any time of the day, week or year. We can understand flows of people and concentrations of behavior. With social media and surveys, we can compare real-time and historical perceptions, allowing a better understanding of how people view their places. We can monitor law enforcement activities and police patrols using spatial technologies to help judge resulting solutions to crime problems. Now, the picture related to data is not completely rosy, as there are excesses and distortions that can come with systematically biased, improperly managed, or inadequately analyzed data (Ferguson 2017). But the data revolution has made an important impact on all aspects of life in modern society, and its role in policing has been dramatic. The positive contributions of data to crime prevention and risk reduction provide an important subtext to risk-based policing.

RISK-BASED POLICING

The advent of risk-based policing does not start a new era unrelated to ideas and practices that have led up to this point in time. In considering the issues of crime analysis, risk, and big data, we need to start with an understanding of the origins of policing and its progression to the modern era. Risk-based policing is an evolution, not a revolution, and its impacts are likely to advance policing only if we understand how we have come to the current state of affairs. Basic expectations and responsibilities of police will be documented in our review of the evolution of police up to the current century. This history of policing, presented in chapter 2, is the starting-off point to provide context to our ideas

FIGURE 1
Steps of risk-based policing.

of integrating new information and modern analysis methods into the policing profession and public safety practice. We are hopeful that a consequence of this advocacy will be a shift in attitudes about the role police officers play in managing public safety and solving crime problems through risk governance and strategic partnerships with members of the communities they serve. Ultimately, risk-based policing is as simple as 1–2-3. As shown in figure 1, risk-based policing requires repeated cycles of (1) assessing environmental risks, crime patterns, and event contexts; (2) deploying people and resources to areas that need them most, then implementing risk reduction strategies at these places; and (3) checking for success by measuring desired outcomes in ways that inform the next round of risk assessments and deployments.

The ideas of risk-based policing are well imbedded in the theoretical approaches to crime analysis that criminologists, data analysts, and legal scholars have developed over the years. This lead-up serves as the bridge that we use for turning research into practice. Not only are we committed to explaining the ways in which risk-based policing with RTM can be used for risk governance, but we also strongly believe that we need to get all the elements of the process working correctly, and to address the pitfalls posed by poor data, improperly formulated research questions, and false conclusions. So, we spend some time in this book explaining our efforts at investigating new ways of analyzing data, selecting target areas, developing risk reduction strategies, presenting outcomes, and offering conclusions in ways that can be easily understood and made actionable by police agencies who want to engage in this enterprise.

CONCLUSION

In this chapter, we introduced the concept of risk-based policing, which addresses the contexts in which crime occurs and helps police focus on the underlying factors that contribute to these undesirable outcomes. This approach turns attention away from individuals and the clustering of their activities in hot spots and toward risky places that promote and support criminal behavior. These behavior settings can be defined by the combined spatial influences of environmental features that enhance the probability of crime, measured through the deployment of RTM to analyze the abundant spatial data now available to law enforcement agencies. Through the development of risk narratives, informed by empirical analysis, police can develop strategies for intervention and long-term crime prevention. In addition, using a risk perspective, they can evaluate the impact of their actions and develop sustainable programs to continue the positive outcomes of their crime reduction strategies. These evidence-based approaches can be shared with community members to advance collaborative problem-solving that involves stakeholders from many different backgrounds in addressing public safety issues.

In the next chapter we delve into a short overview of the history of policing, from the progressive era up to the modern day, as a way of contextualizing the role that evidence-based approaches play in crime prevention and problem solving. This sets the foundation for our more detailed presentation of the ways in which risk-based policing builds on past policing practices and offers a way to extend crime prevention successes while overcoming the challenges.

2

THE EVOLUTION OF MODERN POLICING

> **KEY POINTS**
> - Policing has historically been subject to major innovations, most notably with the establishment of the professional era of policing that formed the basis for current police management structures and procedures.
> - Evaluation of police strategies has demonstrated mixed success in advancing law enforcement practice through the professional model, but recent efforts to open police to evidence-based procedures have resulted in improvements in crime prevention outcomes.
> - Advances have been made through recent incorporation of modern technology and big data in crime forecasting.
> - Risk reduction strategies encourage police to experiment with more place-based interventions to overcome the complaints about overly aggressive, person-focused policing.

INTRODUCTION

The history of policing is bookmarked by distinct points in time that brought about significant changes in the mission and strategy of police. Whereas policing was once a highly politicized, ineffective institution, now there exists a great deal of empirical evidence demonstrating the ability of police to prevent crime and promote public safety. This transformation was made possible by a willingness of police leaders to adopt strategic innovations during particular times of crisis. The evolution of policing accelerated by crisis-catalyzed reforms and watershed moments is noteworthy, as innovations in the field vastly outpaced most other criminal justice institutions (Skogan and Frydl 2004). Nonetheless, contemporary policing is far from infallible, and there is certainly room for continued innovation and improvement.

Several scholars have argued that policing now finds itself in another era of crisis, with high-profile police use-of-force events highlighting rifts in the relationship between police and citizens, particularly in minority communities. In addition, while we have a body of evidence regarding the effects of general police strategies, much less is settled regarding the precise actions police officers should take when engaged in operational practices. While research has found that focusing officer deployment in geographic crime hot spots reduces crime, a review of the literature suggests that "what exactly police should be doing in crime hot spots remains an open question" (Haberman 2016, 489). Yet, what officers do in hot spots has great importance, because policing tactics have the potential of alienating communities in need, regardless of their real or perceived crime prevention utility (Sweeten 2016). In addition, while the identification of hot spots and subsequent deployments of resources to such areas is an increasingly common practice in contemporary policing, much less work has been done to contextualize hot spots. While criminologists have dedicated effort to identifying geographic features associated with hot spots (Bernasco and Block 2011; Caplan, Kennedy, and Miller 2011; Kennedy, Caplan, and Piza 2011), much less attention has been paid to developing crime prevention strategies that are tailored to the contextual features of these environments. Police have historically focused interventions on the people located within hot spot areas in an effort to remove certain ones to prevent criminal opportunity. For example, the treatment prescribed for hot spot areas in New York City in the 1990s was a "broken windows" style of policing whereby lower-level offenses were given higher priority and police officers were mandated to measure productivity and demonstrate success on the job by stopping, frisking, citing, and arresting individuals located in spatially defined problem areas. Ultimately, minority communities bore the brunt of this focused attention and treatment by police. Simmering frustrations and frayed relations between police and the public they serve are exacerbated when crime-analysis products fail to elucidate root attractors of illegal behavior, especially when responses to spatial intelligence fail to acutely address the qualities of places and fail to look beyond merely the people located there.

Policing may currently find itself in another moment ripe for innovation. It may be inaccurate to label current times a "crisis" on par with the civil unrest of the 1960s or the rise of the crack epidemic and related violence in the late 1980s and early 1990s. Still, events of the day related to civil unrest and negative reactions of communities to law enforcement actions deemed too harsh or falling too heavily on certain communities point to the need for continued reform and evolution in policing. What is required for such innovation and evolution to take place? In our view, the next round of innovation in policing requires a renewed consideration of the role of crime analysis and criminogenic places in the development of strategies that provide more accountability in policing practices. The rest of this chapter contextualizes the current need for police innovation through a discussion of the history of policing in the United States.

POLICE REFORM AND PROFESSIONALIZATION

While laws governing the delivery of law enforcement are advanced and enacted within different components of the criminal justice system (e.g., state and federal courts), police officers are the agents who most directly engage with the public in the enforcement of laws. As such, police are by far the most visible and personally accessible agents of government (Greene 2000). Due to this conspicuous central role in society, it is easy to forget that, as a social institution, policing is fairly young. Organized police departments emerged less than 200 years ago, when British Home Secretary Robert Peel created London's Metropolitan Police Force, in 1829. American policing was established even more recently, with the first police departments in the United States not emerging until 1838 and 1844, in Boston and New York City, respectively (Reichel 1992). As a means of comparison, Rutgers University, where all three of us are either current faculty or alumni, was established in 1766, over seventy years before the Boston Police Department and a decade before the ratification of the Declaration of Independence. Given the relative youth of policing, it would be a mistake to consider the art and science of policing "mature" at any point in its history (Sparrow, Moore, and Kennedy 1990). Rather, policing is a discipline that has undergone a great deal of change since its infancy, and inevitably continues to evolve.

The nature of policing in the United States is largely contingent on the factors occurring at any given point in history. As described by Jenkins and DeCarlo (2015, 3), "changing social, cultural, economic, and political environments punctuate various elements of policing, thereby altering each era's idea of what constitutes 'policing'." Prior to the formation of the Boston and New York City police departments, colonial America relied on a "watch" system staffed by able-bodied male citizens. Such systems were sufficient for colonial times, as the watch ensured that law enforcement issues of the day, such as providing for the orderly use of public places; maintaining sanitation; controlling liquor, gambling, and vice; and assisting landowners in recovering runaway slaves were readily addressed (Gaines and Kappeler 2005). As watch patrols grew, formal law enforcement positions, including constables and sheriffs, emerged as a means of better organizing and supervising watch functions, as local governments took responsibility for municipal duties such as tax collection, maintaining roads, and conducting elections (Walker and Katz 2005).

In the early 1800s, the changing nature of life in America presented the need for more formally organized police services. Rapid immigration, industrialization, and urbanization presented challenges (and risks) that watch patrols were ill equipped to address. The formation of formal police departments was spurred by a series of riots in the 1830s, which caused extensive property damage, physical injuries, and, in certain cases, death (Gaines and Kappeler 2005; Walker and Katz 2005). Indeed, the Boston and New York City police departments were established soon after riots in the respective cities (Reichel 1992).

Early American policing was vastly unfocused, with police having little idea of the proper roles that should encapsulate crime prevention. Rather, police often assumed responsibility for any and every public problem that arose: providing ambulance services, running soup kitchens, collecting garbage, and sheltering the homeless when needed (Sparrow, Moore, and Kennedy 1990, 34). Early American policing was also inherently corrupt, with political connections and favoritism substituting for any semblance of professional standards (Walker and Katz 2005). The influence of politics in American policing was likely due, at least partially, to their one point of departure from the British model. While American police departments were modeled after the London Metropolitan Police Force, American police leaders were directly appointed and accountable to municipal leadership. This contrasted with the British system, in which police leaders reported directly to a member of the prime minister's cabinet, thus removing them from local politics. The result of having American police leaders under municipal control essentially amounted to police officers serving as "adjuncts to the city political machines" (Fogelson 1977, cited in Sparrow, Moore, and Kennedy 1990, 33).

Early reformers took notice of police inefficiencies and harshly criticized police organizations across three main areas: their purposes and responsibilities, their organizational form, and their accountability (Sparrow, Moore, and Kennedy 1990). In the late 1800s, a series of municipal commissions and other investigations uncovered massive numbers of scandals involving police officers systematically charging offenders fees for not enforcing the law, informal licensing of illegal activities, and oppressive, illegal, and often brutal police tactics (Fogelson 1977). Before long, the issue of police corruption received attention from the public and, to a lesser extent, police leaders. New York City, for example, created the first state-controlled police commission in 1857, with a number of states following suit afterwards (Walker and Katz 2005). While the reform movement made large gains in addressing corruption in policing, the quality of policing was left largely untouched. Standards for recruitment, training, and supervision remained unchanged, and police gave little thought to how they could effectively prevent crime.

The reform movement, led by police chiefs such as August Volmer, O. W. Wilson, and William Parker, ushered in the professional era of policing with a renewed emphasis on police effectiveness. The professional era largely modeled the American policing industry into its current form. A paramilitary hierarchy was quickly adopted, with operational arrangements emphasizing the power of police headquarters (Wilson 1963). The professional era also established a new set of operational priorities that arguably remain the pillars of policing to this day. First, automobile patrol replaced foot patrol as the main operational strategy of police. The move from foot to automobile was generated by several perceived benefits, specifically that automobiles increased the amount of geography an officer could cover, allowed officers to keep pace with criminals (who increasingly used cars in their offenses), and enabled officers to respond rapidly to reported crime. This idea of rapid response became entrenched in the professional model of policing with the advent of the 9-1-1 emergency call line and two-way radios. The 9-1-1 system essentially meant that the public could easily report victimization to police, and officers would be notified in a timely manner and deploy to the scene. While waiting for such notification, police officers were able to keep patrolling the street, thus maintaining their perceived "omnipresence," which reformers considered the key to deterrence. The latter stages of the professional movement also emphasized retroactive criminal investigations. The status of investigators was greatly enhanced when J. Edgar Hoover took control of the FBI in the 1920s and, through a variety of measures, created what was widely considered an incorruptible and proficient FBI (Reppetto 1978). The prestige of Hoover and the FBI led American municipal police agencies to design their own investigative practices after the FBI model, which involved teams of detectives conducting ad hoc investigations to hold offenders accountable in the hopes of generating deterrence through arrests (Braga et al. 2011).

American policing came under great scrutiny and pressure by the late 1960s. To be clear, social unrest in the 1960s had an impact on the country well outside of policing. The civil rights movement highlighted grave inequalities facing Black people in American society. This decade also saw the public assassinations of prominent champions of civil rights, including Martin Luther King Jr. and President John F. Kennedy. The civil disturbances underlying the events of the decade culminated in a series of riots. In 1967 alone, 128 disturbances occurred in cities across the United States, including Cincinnati, Detroit, Los Angeles, and Newark. The most destructive of these riots, which occurred in Detroit, resulted in 43 deaths and over 7,000 arrests (Tuttle 2009, 168). In addition to civil unrest, crime levels began a significant upward trend starting in the 1960s. This crime increase led to a widespread belief among Americans that the criminal justice system, especially in regard to the police, was failing to ensure adequate public safety (Weisburd and Braga 2006).

President Lyndon B. Johnson, largely motivated by rising crime and widespread civil unrest, established the President's Commission on Law Enforcement and Administration of Justice. In its final report, *The Challenge of Crime in a Free Society* (1967), the commission advocated rectifying the "root causes" of crime, which were largely based in societal ills. The emphasis on social ills was highlighted by recommendations of the commission to move certain offenses out of the realm of police. For example, the commission recommended the decriminalization of drunkenness, arguing that this problem could be better addressed if treated as a public health issue rather than a crime (Klofas, Hipple, and McGarrell 2010). The president's commission also emphasized the importance of police discretion and training officers on how to better navigate interactions with citizens (Kelling and Coles 1996, 179).

At first glance, the recommendations of the commission seem to have provided impetus for moving beyond the strategies of the professional era. However, the commission's report and subsequent public policy had the opposite effect, with the strategies of the professional era becoming even more entrenched. This was partly due to the commission's insistence on labeling police as "law enforcement" and the "gatekeepers" of the criminal justice system (Kelling and Coles 1996; Klofas, Hipple, and McGarrell 2010). This view of police helped foster a warrior image of police that arguably endures to this day (Rahr and Rice 2015).

In 1968, in response to the commission's findings, the U.S. Congress passed the Omnibus Crime Control and Safe Streets Act. The omnibus bill greatly enhanced the Law Enforcement Assistance Administration (LEAA), which established the Office of Law Enforcement Assistance to award grants and administer other programs aimed at improving and expanding law enforcement, court administration, and prison operations at the state and local levels. State governments, granted great leeway in determining how to distribute funds, emphasized law enforcement solutions over addressing the "root causes" of crime or improving police training (Travis, Western, and Redburn 2014, chap. 4). By a wide margin, LEAA funding primarily enabled projects to purchase police equipment, such as vehicles and weapons, many of which were adapted from military equipment previously used in the Vietnam War (Varon 1975).

The 1960s and 1970s were met with a drastic lack of confidence in the police on the part of the American public (LaFree 1998). The scientific community questioned the predominant tactics of the professional era, which would come to be known as the "standard model" of policing. An increase in funding for police research, in the form of grants from the National Institute of Law Enforcement and Criminal Justice (which would later become the National Institute of Justice) and private foundations, such as the Ford Foundation, led to an influx of studies on the standard model of policing (Weisburd and Braga 2006). This body of academic inquiry found little support for the approaches police had committed themselves to for decades, including preventive patrol (Kelling et al. 1974), rapid response to calls for service (Kansas City, Missouri, Police Department 1977; Spelman and Brown 1981), and retroactive investigations (Greenwood et al. 1977; Eck 1983). Systematic reviews of research evidence (Sherman and Eck 2002; Skogan and Frydl 2004; Weisburd and Eck 2004) confirmed that popular strategies of the professional era were largely ineffective. To be fair, many of these studies overstated the policy implications of their findings (Weisburd and Braga 2006; Weisburd and Eck 2004), and there has been little replication of these evaluations in recent times (Skogan and Frydl 2004). Nonetheless, there is wide consensus that the standard model of policing provides little value in terms of crime prevention (Skogan and Frydl 2004; Sherman and Eck 2002; Weisburd and Eck 2004).

FROM PROFESSIONALISM TO PROBLEM-SOLVING

In light of the mounting evidence undercutting support for the standard model of policing, scholars and practitioners began conceptualizing and implementing new strategies for crime prevention. These strategies, which would collectively come to be known as the "focused model" of policing (Skogan and Frydl 2004), each emerged as alternatives to the standard model and the widespread recognition of the policing crisis manifest in the 1960s and 1970s (Weisburd and Braga 2006). The contrast between such contemporary practices and the standard model of policing was well articulated by Herman Goldstein (1979) in his seminal article, "Improving Policing: A Problem-Oriented Approach," which foreshadowed the emergence of an alternative approach to police practice. Goldstein argued that traditional policing suffered from a "means over ends syndrome" that placed more emphasis on the organizational structure and operating methods than on the substantive outcome of their work. Goldstein argued that this resulted in an incident-based approach, whereby departments respond to individual incidents (many involving the same places and actors) instead of solving recurring problems that generate these crime incidents in the first place. As an alternative, Goldstein developed "problem-oriented policing," advocating that police systematically identify and analyze the underlying problems generating crime and devise solutions specifically tailored to alleviate said problems. By the time Goldstein expanded on these ideas in his book *Problem-Oriented Policing* (1990), a number of strategic innovations in policing had been advanced, including hot spots policing (Sherman, Gartin, and Buerger 1989), broken windows (Wilson and Kelling 1982), community policing (Skogan 1990), and situational crime prevention (Clarke and Mayhew 1980). These tactics were soon followed by the development of strategies like focused deterrence (Kennedy 1997), evidence-based policing (Sherman 1998), and third-party policing (Buerger and Mazerolle 1998).

Despite their unique approaches to crime and criminals, all of these innovations had certain commonalities. First, these strategies emphasize the importance of police working proactively to address crime problems rather than simply reacting to crime occurrence, as in the standard model. As explained by Wu and Lum (2016, 1–2), police proactivity is not a singular action, but rather includes a "wide gamut of activities intended mostly to prevent and deter crime and recidivism." This diversity of activities shares the overall goal of managing the threat of crime through proactive actions. Proactively addressing problems of concern allows police to focus officer attention on the problem at hand, which research suggests generates substantial reductions in crime, particularly when interventions include an array of diverse responses (Weisburd and Eck 2004).

Second, most contemporary police strategies rely heavily on crime analysis during the design and implementation stages of the intervention. The rate of change and innovation in policing has outpaced virtually all other government entities, with the police reconsidering their fundamental mission and many of their core strategies in a relatively short period (Weisburd and Braga 2006). In many ways, crime analysts have been front and center in this strategic evolution. Certain strategies, such as hot spots policing, cannot occur without the work of crime analysts, as the identification of hot spots is a prerequisite for target-area identification and resource allocation. Crime analysis is also essential for other policing strategies, such as problem-oriented policing, pulling levers, intelligence-led policing, and predictive policing (see Santos 2014, 163, table 1.). While crime analysis does not replace the work and skills of sworn police personnel, it is designed to complement and add value to that work. Indeed, Santos (2013b) found that the incorporation of rigorous crime analysis in the daily functions of all levels of a police agency was associated with significant crime reductions in Port St. Lucie, Florida. In this sense, the emergence of crime analysis can be considered a driving force in the modern evolution of policing.

THE IMPORTANCE OF PLACES AND DATA ANALYSIS IN CONTEMPORARY POLICING

In discussing modern policing, it is important to note the renewed emphasis on the role of place in crime prevention. To be clear, police have always focused on "places" in certain regards, as police services (e.g. patrol) have traditionally been organized and delivered according to specific units of geography, such as sectors or precincts (Weisburd 2008). However, the problem with measuring crime problems according to predetermined administrative boundaries derives from the fact that such boundaries are typically drawn for the convenience of service delivery and may be poor representations of crime clusters relating to public safety (Piza, Caplan, and Kennedy 2014). Therefore, problems residing in shapes and dimensions not reflected in such units of analysis are unlikely to be sufficiently measured though these analytical processes (Sparrow 2016, 126). In that sense, modern policing has reconsidered the notion of place to mean very small, micro units of analysis, such as block faces or street segments (Eck and Weisburd 1995; Weisburd 2008), assuming that these better represent the scale at which public safety problems reside. With this change came a renewed interest in the theoretical perspectives assigning criminality to certain typologies of locales, specifically the theories of environmental criminology: routine activities (Cohen and Felson 1979), rational choice (Cornish and Clarke 1986), crime pattern theory (Brantingham and Brantingham 1993), and the theory of risky places (Kennedy et al. 2016). While some studies have found that crime analysts may not always introduce the concepts of environmental criminology into the work of police departments (Wartell and Gallagher 2012), contemporary police practices have increasingly focused on place. Sparrow (2011) has noted that the evidence-based policing movement is dominated by evaluations of place-based responses to crime. Even strategies not exclusively concerned with geographic hot spots, such as problem-oriented and offender-based strategies, often incorporate concise geographies as units of analysis (e.g. Braga et al. 1999; Groff et al. 2015; Weisburd et al. 2010). While Sparrow (2011) argued that an over-emphasis on place might lead researchers to overlook pertinent crime problems not attributable to specific geographies, it is important to note that the central role of place in policing is likely due to the observed success of place-based policing strategies. The Committee to Review Research on Police Policy and Practices (Skogan and Frydl 2004) found that geographically focused strategies had the strongest record of effect, with a more recently published systematic review and meta-analysis similarly supporting this finding (Braga, Papachristos, and Hureau 2014).

Let us now revisit the role of crime analysis, specifically in a policing paradigm highly committed to place-based strategies. As previously discussed, crime analysis has been invaluable to the development of contemporary police strategies. However, a review of the literature suggests that there is room for improvement in the manner by which police analyze crime problems. For example, while research has found problem-oriented policing (POP) to be associated with significant crime reductions (Weisburd et al. 2010), scholars have noted that the contemporary use of POP rarely adheres to the SARA (scanning, analysis, response, assessment) model that POP is built upon (Clarke 1998; Sparrow 2016). Many POP efforts can be accurately classified as "shallow problem solving" (Braga and Weisburd 2006) whereby officers conduct superficial analyses of problems and resort to traditional law enforcement tactics (e.g., arrests, stop-and-frisks, knock-and-talks, serving warrants) rather than incorporating a more horizontal approach that directly addresses the underlying problems (Read and Tilley 2000). Community policing has similarly been implemented in a reduced form, often relegated to specialized units rather than practiced on a department-wide basis as originally intended (Mastrofski 2006; Sparrow 2016).

Similar issues have been observed regarding CompStat, the data-driven approach to police management, strategy development, and performance assessment popularized in the 1990s. When initially developed by the NYPD, CompStat adhered to four main principles: accurate and timely intelligence; rapid deployment; effective tactics; and relentless follow-up and assessment (Maple and Mitchell 1999). While the NYPD's original intent with CompStat was to enhance their problem-solving capacity (Bratton and Knobler 1998; Silverman 2006), later efforts in New York City and elsewhere placed disproportionate emphasis on the "relentless follow-up and assessment" principle (Eterno and Silverman 2012). This shift in focus translated to a process in which "analysis" rarely strayed beyond the tallying of crime counts across precincts and temporal periods and the comparison of binary crime counts from the current time period with a preceding time period (typically from the prior year). Such analysis diminished the role of problem-solving in favor of strategies that reinforced standard police responses and the bureaucratic models of police organization (Bond and Braga 2013; Weisburd et al. 2003). As articulated by Sparrow (2016, 119), police have largely implemented CompStat programs as "de facto substitutes for any broader problem-solving approach, thereby restricting or narrowing both the types of problems police can address and the range of solutions they are able to consider." In addition, the simple presentation of two crime totals does not sufficiently communicate trends or trajectories, but encourages decision-makers to interpret any differences (no matter how small) as precise and meaningful (Guilfoyle 2015). The end result is police commanders making unwarranted assumptions, not controlling for uncertainties, and taking disproportionate operational responses in the light of minor, and often insignificant, differences in crime counts (Guilfoyle 2015).

As demonstrated in the preceding paragraph, a main problem with superficial analysis of crime problems is that subsequent responses by police may be similarly limited in scope. Police strategies focusing attention on places nicely illustrate this issue. Again, research has consistently shown that crimes cluster at specific locations (Sherman, Gartin, and Buerger 1989), with such clustering persisting over extensive time periods in certain cases (Braga, Papachristos, and Hureau 2010; Schnell, Braga, and Piza 2016; Weisburd et al. 2004; Wheeler, Mclean, and Worden 2016). Given that crimes cluster spatially, many have rightly argued that crime prevention resources "should be similarly concentrated rather than diffused across urban areas" to achieve maximum impact (Braga, Papachristos, and Hureau 2010, 34). We previously discussed the benefits of place-based strategies, and we should also mention that they offer a more efficient method of policing than offender-based strategies. While places often demonstrate relatively stable crime levels over time, it is well established that individuals experience both short-term and long-term variations in criminal propensity (Agnew 2011). Weisburd (2008, 6), for example, noted that police in Seattle would have to target four times as many people as places to account for 50 percent of the crime incidents that occurred between 1989 and 2002.

While hot spot mapping has allowed police to more effectively target criminogenic places, the nature of the social and physical environments of hot spots has received less attention in the design of police interventions. In Cohen and Felson's (1979) original article on routine activities, they wrote that "the risk of criminal victimization varies dramatically among the circumstances and locations in which people place themselves and their property" (595). It would seem that motivated offenders commit crime against suitable targets at certain places according to the environmental characteristics of those places, making it easier to complete the crime successfully and reap the rewards without punishment (i.e., getting caught). Therefore, the context of high-crime places should be incorporated into police responses. Unfortunately, this has yet to occur on a widespread basis. This may be partly related to the analytical products commonly used in the creation of place-based interventions. Hot spot maps, for instance, show the concentration of crime but offer little in the sense of physical structure. Such focus on a single variable (e.g., crime incident locations) is akin to what Reboussin, Warren, and Hazelwood (1995) refer to as a "mapless map." As explained by Rengert and Lockwood (2009, 109), "A mapless map is a mere description since it describes how one variable is distributed in space. . . . In order to determine 'why' it is distributed the way it is, the spatial distribution of at least one other variable needs to be considered."

The result of "mapless maps" has been hot spots policing strategies that are largely one-dimensional, promoting the concentration of resources in high-crime places. Little thought has been given to how police activities can mitigate features of the places that attract illegal behaviors or give rise to crime. As argued by Braga (2015, 17), "Too many police departments seem to rely on over-simplistic tactics, such as 'putting cops on dots' or launching indiscriminate zero-tolerance initiatives rather than engaging a coherent crime prevention strategy." Even the recently emerging field of predictive policing is, in reality, based on traditional law enforcement methods. Predictive policing refers to the use of analytic methods dedicated to predicting when and where crime is most likely to occur (Perry et al. 2013). As argued by Sparrow (2016, 100–01), "For anyone familiar with crime analysis, this is not new. And it is particularly not new when the default intervention strategy involves putting cops on dots." Indeed, most predictive policing efforts much more resemble hot spots policing than a new strategy (Sklansky 2011). Jeffrey Brantingham, one of the founders of a predictive policing software company, explained that in response to the place-based predictions, officers are vaguely instructed to use their "knowledge, skills, experience and training in the most appropriate way to stop crime" (Huet 2015). This ambiguity about what to do at crime hot spots is not surprising, but rather follows a consistent theme in policing, as technological advancements have often been used to reinforce established analytic and tactical approaches rather than to develop new approaches. Over a six-year study period, Manning (2008) found that crime mapping and information technology were never used to call existing strategies into question, but rather adapted to support current practices.

How can the scope of place-based policing practices be expanded, particularly in a manner that more readily incorporates the structure of criminogenic places? The answer, at least partially, may lie in the analytical products produced in support of intervention development. As argued by Sparrow (2016, 126–27), "The only way to break out of this circularity trap—where operational methods determine what analyses are commissioned, and the analyses conducted determine the types of problems that are detected—is to throw wide open the analytic operation and demand much greater versatility. . . . By deliberately increasing the versatility of the analytic operation, the organization increases the range of problems it can detect. Discovering new types of problems, in turn, then challenges the organization to develop relevant and novel operational responses." To be clear, current analytical products seem to be serving police well, given the aforementioned discussion of the crime prevention utility of place-based approaches. However, recent events highlight the importance of judging police responses not just according to crime changes, but also in terms of efficiency, equity, and cost-effectiveness. Risk terrain modeling's ability to diagnose high-crime places, offering in-depth understanding of how structural and social factors interact to facilitate crime emergence (Kennedy et al. 2016), goes a long way toward expanding the scope of place-based policing. This is why risk terrain modeling is a key element of risk-based policing.

CONCLUSION

An examination of the policing literature reveals an institution constantly undergoing changes in its core strategy and mission. To their credit, police agencies have readily sought out evidence-based approaches by incorporating crime-analysis techniques and findings of rigorous program evaluations in developing new strategies. While it would be inaccurate to claim that crime prevention policies are completely devoid of political influence (see e.g. Papachristos 2011), contemporary police strategies are largely rooted in criminological theory and research evidence.

We believe that the history of policing, as outlined in this chapter, suggests that we find ourselves at the cusp of a new era of policing. Current events suggest a need to refine the scope of place-based policing as well as the analytical techniques used to devise such strategies. In the next chapters, we present our model of risk-based policing, which uses risk terrain modeling to build upon prior crime-and-place studies in a manner enabling a more nuanced understanding of the contextual aspects of high-crime places and more holistic, effective, and sustainable approaches to crime prevention (Caplan and Kennedy 2016).

3

POLICING IN THE NEW ERA OF PUBLIC SAFETY AND LAW ENFORCEMENT

> **KEY POINTS**
>
> - Risk terrain modeling (RTM) allows police to diagnose features of a landscape that interact to create unique behavior settings with increased vulnerability to crime.
> - RTM complements hot spot and other analysis methods in identifying locations where crime is likely to occur because of risky features of the landscape that deserve greater police attention.
> - RTM enables assessments of some places relative to others and serves to develop risk narratives that inform decisions about what to do at places that repeatedly attract illegal behavior, to mitigate their appeal to offenders.
> - Risk-based policing with RTM extends police work beyond specific deterrence and arrests to community problem-solving and crime prevention.

FOCUS ON PLACES WITH RISK TERRAIN MODELING

As we discussed in chapter 2, police have traditionally responded to crime incidents, and where they occur most often, rather than understanding why they frequently occur and what is attracting or generating crimes at certain places over and over again. Criminals directly and indirectly communicate preferences of spatial attractors and event contexts through their illegal actions, so their patterns of illegal behavior can be studied to anticipate new crime locations. RTM allows police to conduct such an analysis to diagnose what features of a landscape interact and overlap to create unique behavior settings and contexts for crime. As a method of spatial analysis, and as discussed in detail in the book *Risk Terrain Modeling: Crime Prediction and Risk Reduction* (Caplan and Kennedy 2016), RTM refers to three key processes: standardizing disparate datasets to a common geography, diagnosing spatial risk factors, and articulating spatial vulnerabilities. The first is a cartographic process of operationalizing qualities of a landscape to geographic maps. These map layers represent the spatial influences of environmental factors across places. *Spatial influence* refers to the way in which features of an environment affect behaviors at or around the features themselves. The second is a statistical process of identifying and weighting factors that geographically relate to crime incidents. The third is a cartographic process whereby the spatial influences of these environmental factors are combined to communicate information about spatial contexts for crime. RTM offers a statistically valid way to articulate vulnerable places at the micro level. Risk scores of places derived from RTM do not suggest the inevitability of crime. Instead, they point to locations where the likelihood of criminal behavior will be high.[1] The predictive validity of RTM has been proven many times by a variety of professionals, and generalized for various crime types and study areas. RTM has become a valuable and insightful tool for police agencies to analyze local crime problems and understand why crime occurs at specific places (Kennedy, Caplan, and Piza 2015). Knowing where and why the underlying problems emerge and persist over time provides opportunities to align prevention services, not only law enforcement activities, to the areas that need them most.

RTM builds on principles of environmental criminology and problem-oriented policing to produce maps that show where conditions are ideal for crimes to occur given existing environmental contexts. It examines the emergence of crime hot spots formed by near-repeats that occur in particular places. The fact that most crimes occur in a few places is important as it allows police to move away from a professional-era strategy of providing equal resources to all areas of a city to one that concentrates resources in the areas where the crime problems are most clustered or severe. However, a major dilemma faced by hot spots policing is that it is not a sustainable analytical method because if crime is reduced enough, there will not be enough data to permit future analyses. And, it cannot account for police success at preventing crimes. When police suppress crime from a particular area, the hot spot disappears, and there is no longer an indicator available for assessing the risk of future crime. Also, when crime does not disappear, the repeated activity of police in hot spots keeps them hot simply because of their law enforcement actions at these locations. Meanwhile, knowledge of a near-repeat phenomenon provides a basis for the police to extend their radius of prevention and enforcement out from a band of crime incidents to areas close by, aiming to reduce the chance of more crime. But, of course, the factors that made the areas susceptible to the first crime incident and that extend to other nearby places remain unknown and unaddressed in any systematic way.

RTM extends the investigation from the crime incidents to the spatial contexts in which these incidents emerge or persist, offering the analytical assessment needed to inform police decision-making. If crimes cluster in hot spots, it is likely that they occur because risk factors that tie to this crime also cluster. RTM provides the framework for diagnosing these factors. Knowing what spatial risks are connected to crime allows the analyst to anticipate future crimes in an area, even if crime has yet to occur there. RTM also enables a test of the precise nature of crime displacement,[2] when it occurs, and incorporates Bayesian probability into crime analysis, even for rare and low-incidence crime problems or other public safety threats. RTM overcomes the event-dependent nature of hot spot mapping and emphasizes the likelihood of crime outcomes based on a calculation of the interactions of spatial risk factors. Risk-based policing operationalizes these assessments and mobilizes resources at key places to mitigate the risks.

RTM has been used in a number of different settings, in urban, suburban, and rural jurisdictions, to analyze different crime types, from drug, property, and violent crimes to international trafficking. These studies have demonstrated how risk terrain maps articulate micro-level places where conditions are suitable for illegal behavior and most likely for crimes to occur. Further, RTM has been shown to articulate officers' "gut" feelings and perceptions of risk at places, beyond merely referencing past occurrences of reported crimes. It also provides a way of analyzing the data generated from complaint lines, such as 3-1-1 calls, or in real time via social media. As an example, the public may call about lights being out in an area, which may foretell a pattern of increased risk of walking through certain places. RTM provides a way to monitor the temporal changes that occur in other locations as the municipality works to rectify the problems and restore working lights in a high-risk area. RTM provides an indication of what risk factors might be at the root of crime problems and thus helps police devise a solution. In this way, RTM helps make information that comes from complaints about problem areas actionable and relevant to service delivery and public safety. While the public may not in themselves have the ability to stop graffiti from happening, street lights from burning out, or housing vacancies spreading through foreclosures, they can complain about these situations. These location-based complaints can serve as a proxy for decline and offer a new perspective on the patterns of risky locations for crime. Social media provides another form of data that can be inputted into RTM and used to identify behavior patterns or the ways in which people evaluate the safety and security of the places they visit. Combining RTM results with social media posts allows police to add context and priorities to the information that is gleaned from various sources, and provides an ongoing dialog about how different groups respond to the locations that they inhabit or travel through.

Researchers and practitioners in most states in the United States and many countries throughout the world use RTM. Probably the greatest challenge to the international initiatives has been researchers' access to valid and reliable data. There are many reasons for this, but the most basic appears to be the concern on the part of authorities that manage these data that privacy will be breached if micro-level data are shared. This has led to counter-pressure from analysts concerning the importance of access to this information. In some jurisdictions, authorities have responded by allowing analysts to operate in secure facilities, restricting their ability to take data with them. There are even some locations in which the data are stored in lead-lined rooms to protect against microwave readers. This treatment of data as highly sensitive is in stark contrast to the tactics now used by most U.S.-based police agencies, which put their crime data online to be downloaded by anyone interested in analyzing it. The rationale behind secretive data practices is a tangential discussion. For now we need to convey how, according to research that has been conducted to date in different locations, data restriction has impacted crime analysis, and what the analysts who face these limitations have done to overcome these hurdles.

The consequence for crime analysis in data-restrictive nations has been to severely limit transparency in the decisions that are made by police. Walls around police data limit what the public are able to know about the consequences of policing actions, despite the availability of aggregated information provided in crime reports on a regular basis. In addition, data restrictions have prevented some researchers from studying place-based phenomena in a way that allows them to focus attention on problem places, beyond what is offered to them in aggregate terms.

When used with micro-level data, RTM enables analysis and problem-solving to become key aspects of policing, where it identifies problem places and also indicates what to focus on when police officers get there. Spatial intelligence informs strategies for actualizing situational crime prevention, pinpointed to specific places. Policing operations focus on the risky places. The risk terrain that is produced allows police to examine the patterns of choices that individuals make about their locations, sort of a "collective offender memory" map that depicts areas with attractive qualities for crime and higher likelihoods of criminal behavior. While RTM may support reasonable application of suspicions and stops, it also facilitates an approach to policing that targets the locations themselves.

It may seem reasonable that targeting individual offenders at risky places would remove the chance of a recurrence of crime and reduce its rate. But police leaders know that vulnerable environments need to be reformed to effectively prevent crime, or else new offenders will take the place of the old. When police rely exclusively on deterrence and incapacitation at high-crime areas, it is rarely effective or equitable. Legal scholars (Koss, 2015; Ferguson, 2012) have explained that risk-based policing with RTM offers an "exceptional opportunity" to quantify target areas in ways that respect constitutional protections for community populations. This, they have said, is because RTM enables a concerted effort to not only focus on individual offenders present in locations at any given moment in time, but to understand and address the mechanisms that enable crime incidents to emerge and persist. RTM enables assessments of some places relative to others and serves to develop risk narratives that inform decisions about what to do at places that repeatedly attract illegal behavior, to mitigate their appeal. Risk narratives are discussed in more detail later in this chapter. Risk-based policing uses these quantifiable outputs to inform strategies that both enhance public safety efforts and safeguard civil rights. With RTM, the focus of risk-based policing is on places, not only people, to prevent crime.

THE CENTRAL TENETS OF RISK-BASED POLICING

Policing encompasses a wide range of activities carried out by police officers to control the affairs of a community, especially with respect to maintenance of order, law, health, safety, and other matters affecting public welfare. *Law enforcement* is a key function of policing, but refers specifically to enforcing the written rules governing society by discovering, deterring, stopping, and/or seizing people who violate the law. While policing and law enforcement affect public safety, *public safety* refers more broadly to the general welfare and protection of the public from various dangers affecting persons, property, and collective well-being. These distinctions among policing, law enforcement, and public safety are important for understanding the missions of modern police agencies and the five central tenets of risk-based policing, which are:

- Focus on places, not only people, to prevent crime (discussed in the prior section of this chapter);
- Develop spatial risk narratives;
- Solicit and value input from all ranks of police personnel and other community stakeholders, including, as much as possible, residents, business owners, and municipal and elected officials, about situational crime contexts, data management, expected outcomes, and performance measures;
- Make data-driven decisions following a transparent process of problem definition, information gathering, and analysis; and
- Balance the real needs and expectations for law enforcement activities with comprehensive strategies for crime risk reduction and public safety.

DEVELOP SPATIAL RISK NARRATIVES

Crime events occur within spatial and situational contexts. In Atlantic City, NJ, which we will discuss in more depth in part 2, stakeholders created risk narratives from RTM results: they believed shootings are probably connected to drug sales and related turf conflicts whereby convenience stores are the places where drug buyers are solicited; nearby laundromats are locations where drug transactions are made; and vacant buildings nearby are used by drug dealers as stash houses for drugs and weapons, or by drug buyers to use drugs after purchase. When community stakeholders used the data-driven evidence to surmise that drugs, prostitution, retail businesses, and vacant properties are related in this way to shootings, they were more likely to agree with police that certain places will probably experience shooting incidents in the future. This led to conversations about how to effectively target and remediate the problems in these locations. In this example, policing interventions aimed at reducing shooting events focused preemptively on factors beyond the shooting incidents, the offenders, or their victims. Areas around laundromats received directed police patrols; police officer "meet-and-greets" with convenience store managers were implemented at frequent intervals every shift; and the city's Planning and Development Department prioritized remediation of vacant properties and installation of new LED street lights (to replace dimmer halogen lamps) at the highest-risk places.

Risk narratives such as this aid police in articulating crime problems in diverse ways, beyond those entailed in established paradigms, practices, or procedures. This supports reasoning with hypotheses, whereby preconceived notions held by police or other stakeholders about the crime problem and its relationships to space and time are tested and addressed accordingly. Police and policy-makers have evidence from RTM to articulate explanations for the occurrence of crime events at any moment in time in ways that diminish assumptions based on high-profile cases or the reinforcement of personal biases accrued from personal experiences or gut feelings. Risk terrain models serve as a foundation for discussions to form and advance risk narratives, to identify new data inputs for inclusion in future analyses, and to propose solutions that can be tested with actions that are planned and implemented to address or disrupt the risk narratives in meaningful and measurable ways. Risk narratives enable effective risk governance led by police and supported by other stakeholders.

SOLICIT AND VALUE INPUT FROM MULTIPLE STAKEHOLDERS

Risk-based policing uses the diagnostic and predictive outputs of RTM to moderate reactive law enforcement actions and maximize resource deployments to places where public safety needs are greatest. It emphasizes problem-solving, evidence-based decision-making, and regular assessments of actions and impacts. Police target offenders for the crimes and harms they commit, and they continue to conduct investigations and clear cases. But police realize they cannot arrest their way out of crime problems; nor should they be expected to try. Many examples of high-crime cities persist with voluminous law enforcement actions, but where the public does not routinely feel safe. Conversely, some cities have seen a drastic cutback on aggressive street-level enforcement without experiencing any significant upticks in crime. New York City, for example, experienced a 93% reduction of stop-question-frisk events from 2011 to 2015 (Ferrandino 2016) without experiencing significant crime increases as a result (see e.g. Pyrooz et al. 2016, fig. 2; Smith 2018). Similar findings have been observed elsewhere, as well (e.g., Shjarback et al. 2017; Towers and White 2017). Thus, it does not appear that aggressive law enforcement on a day-to-day basis inherently equates to public safety. Repeat offenses at the same places label areas "problematic" and garner police attention. But the seizure of an offender (or two, or three, etc.) from a hot spot area rarely diminishes the overall stability of the hot spot in the long term. Policing focused solely on seizing or incapacitating offenders located at hot spots often fails to cool hot spots because unaffected offenders adjust to these inconveniences (i.e., arrests) inflicted on others and continue to be attracted to these settings. Solving crime problems requires a concerted effort not only to focus on the individual offenders or their (potential) victims present there at any given moment in time, but to assess the mechanisms that enable hot spots to emerge and persist. Innovative police leaders recognize this and, through risk-based policing, redefine the missions of their police departments from "policing people in communities" to "governing crime risks while also enforcing the law."

"Our earth is round and, among other things, that means that you and I can hold completely different points of view and both be right," wrote June Jordan (1970), a poet, teacher, and essayist born in Harlem in 1936. "The difference of our positions will show stars in your window I cannot even imagine." Risk-based policing works best when police officials acknowledge the difference of their perspectives on crime relative to various other community stakeholders and all parties realize that their points of view can contribute to achieving the shared goal of public safety. When police share the burden of ensuring public safety with other city agencies and community stakeholders, these people become partners to help solve existing crime problems and to identify and address emerging public safety threats. This keeps police officers safer, too. And it goes a long way toward making policing and related activities effective, sustainable, and less susceptible to bias. Additionally, with an appraisal of risk narratives by police officers and other stakeholders, public safety efforts remain grounded in the nuanced social, cultural, economic, and political atmospheres in which crime is happening. The most vocal or politically connected constituents, for instance, don't get intervention efforts in their neighborhoods first if these places are not the highest-risk. This articulable and justifiable response prioritization is a valuable commodity for elected officials who must allocate limited resources in transparent ways.

This was demonstrated at a community meeting in Jersey City, NJ, when discussions centered on gas stations, identified by the risk terrain model as one of the highest risk factors for violent crimes. RTM confirmed experienced police officers' gut feelings about these locations. But a community stakeholder (from a local youth organization) added context to the conversation that warranted further analysis before interventions were planned. She argued that "service stations," "gas-only stations," and "gas stations with food marts" should not be lumped together in one category (as was originally done). The reasoning, she explained, derived from her awareness of youth hanging out after school around convenience stores, where they can easily congregate and get food and drinks. A city ordinance requires closing time for these business to be 10 P.M., but gas stations with food marts are exempted. The 24-hours-a-day, 7-days-a-week gas stations provide space for youth to congregate late at night, creating unique contexts for victimization. Her well-articulated opinion was reasonable to other stakeholders, and so new data were collected and analyses rerun before decisions about intervention strategies were made. In this example, the social relevancy of environmental features affected their spatial influences on behaviors at different times and under particular circumstances.[3] That is, the attractive qualities and related risks of convenience stores are very different at 10:30 A.M. compared to 10:30 P.M.; school days and weekends can also vary. Interactions among people and their geographies are deeply fluid and something that must be considered by multiple stakeholders with regard to risk governance. RTM diagnoses environmental risk factors, whereas risk narratives help convey their contextual nuances to plan risk reduction strategies that disrupt the criminogenic qualities accordingly.

MAKE DATA-DRIVEN DECISIONS

With risk-based policing, police review RTM reports and define the focus and intent of responsive actions. They record productivity data accordingly and then measure success by clear standards. Ideally, the risk reduction activities suppress a risk factor's attractive qualities completely, rendering it empirically absent from the subsequent risk terrain model altogether. Reported crime rates and the quantification of arrests and citations continue to be important performance measures for some police agencies. But RTM removes the need for a sole dependency on them, and it adds new options. Policing has an important role to play in affecting the risk terrain. Police officers can deter offenders, embolden victims, and assist in the hardening of targets. These products can have the overall impact of reducing crime occurrence. But an effective and sustainable risk reduction strategy requires identifying the environmental conditions in which crime is likely to appear, based on diagnostics from RTM. Then the next step is to propose strategies to address these conditions and interrupt the interactions that lead to illegal behavior settings and crime outcomes. Risk reduction often includes activities related to (1) reducing the spatial influence of one or more environmental risk factors that were identified by RTM; (2) target-hardening, situational prevention, or community awareness; and (3) police patrols or other operations to deter motivated offenders at high-risk places.

Police agencies implementing risk-based policing have been able to emphasize situational approaches to crime prevention in lieu of more traditional law enforcement tactics, such as stop-and-frisk. Thus, risk-based policing presents opportunities to build processes for systematically collecting data relevant to risk-based interventions. As previously discussed, police have traditionally collected data on crime occurrence and police enforcement activity when measuring the success and fidelity of targeted efforts. Given that risk-based policing routinely diagnoses underlying attractors of crime hot spots, this approach lends credence to evaluation efforts incorporating a wider range of data sets. Process and outcome measures are typically operationalized as part of evaluations conducted by outside academic researchers. However, recent research suggests that such data can be readily collected and analyzed by police agencies themselves through the increased use of police "pracademics," active police officers who have received academic research training that they can apply to in-house analytical efforts (Huey and Mitchell

2016). In addition, Piza and Feng (2017) have argued that crime analysis units offer a particularly rich source for evidence-based policing, as demonstrated by the increased reliance on crime-analysis products in the design and implementation of contemporary police practices. Piza and Feng further explained that police would benefit from empowering crime analysts to conduct in-house evaluations of agency programs and practices; provide recommendations related to training; reconfigure CompStat processes; and design researcher–practitioner partnerships around the core components of the action research methodology.

The cumulative effect of risks allows police leaders to develop a reliable probability of crime occurring at certain places over time, during and after interventions. This is accomplished through a comparison of various outcome measures and/or through an analysis that considers treatment and control areas during the same time periods. Sparrow (2015) argues that reported crime rates will always be important indicators for police departments. However, substantial and recurrent reductions in crime figures are only possible when crime problems have first grown out of control. A sole reliance on the metric of crime reduction, Sparrow explained, would "utterly fail" (5) to reflect the very best performance in crime prevention practices when police actions are successful at keeping crime rates low and nipping emerging crime problems as they bud. Beyond looking at crime-rate changes, a risk governance approach to solving crime problems points to success when factors in addition to crime counts improve.

BALANCE STRATEGIES FOR CRIME RISK REDUCTION

Police leaders, such as in Fayetteville, NC, and Atlantic City, NJ, have embraced risk-based policing for their agencies to balance law enforcement activities with strategies for crime risk reduction. As Captain Nolette of the Fayetteville Police Department explained, with RTM and smart policing concepts, police can identify factors that contribute to attracting criminal behavior and develop thoughtful responses to their city's unique circumstances (Nolette 2016). The Fayetteville Police Department reported reduced violent crime citywide by 11 percent. This occurred with minimal disruption to regularly expected patrol functions; no additional resources; and improved rapport with community stakeholders. There was more satisfaction all around. In Atlantic City the value of RTM derives from the fact that it shifts the focus of crime reduction away from people and onto places by using hard data showing that people tend to commit crimes in certain kinds of environments. This is according to Henry White, an old-school cop who started on foot patrol in 1985 and rose through the ranks to become chief of the Atlantic City Police Department. "That's why I like this model so much," White told the attendees of a business luncheon in 2016 (Strenger 2016). It improves community relations and does not define people as the problem, nor does it focus on people as the crime problem's sole fix. "We were able to reduce crime without contributing to mass incarceration," Chief White said (Melamed 2017).

In the Fort Worth area of Texas, police are working in partnership with Cook Children's Hospital to identify risky situations for children in homes during calls-for-service (such as the presence of an infant child but no crib or safe place to sleep in the house) and making referrals to outreach services that can directly provide free cribs and other needed resources (Rice 2017). "It's about changing the context, changing the features of the environment, so the people living there are safe," explained Dr. Dyann Daley (Blackburn 2017). In addition to police efforts toward this goal, non-profits like One Safe Place (an organization that helps abuse victims) are using risk terrain maps to target ad buys and put boots on the ground in high-risk places to help potential victims get out of dangerous situations before abuse occurs. Risk-based policing complements police and other community leaders who have already established programs that bring together police officers and other stakeholders by adding options to what would otherwise be law enforcement responses to people in crisis. Risk-based policing needs the preconceived notions about police being a force of community warriors pitted against bad people to be replaced with a sense of job satisfaction when emergency calls for police services diminish, juxtaposed with positive and strategic police–community interactions increasing at high-risk places.

Risk narratives about the dynamic interactions among people that occur at places can be shared with multiple stakeholders as a way of determining effective strategies for responding to threats and crime outbreaks. In the interactions that take place between crime incidents and context, constantly changing risk dependencies emerge from the actions of all persons and features at locations. It is here that risk-based policing integrates law enforcement, public safety, and community engagement—all focused on risk governance for the purpose of crime prevention—with great effect. "We've had certain neighborhoods in town that have been hot spots since I was on patrol," explained Chief White. "We made a ton of arrests. But, you know what? They were still hot spots until recently. Before, we would clean up an area temporarily but all we were doing was displacing crime" (Melamed 2017). The sustainability of risk-based policing comes from reduced crime plus many other benefits that propagate ground-swelled buy-in and further engagement among police officers and other stakeholders at all levels of the community.

CONCLUSION

The imperatives of risk-based policing require broadening policing practice to go beyond law enforcement and include consideration of the contexts in which crimes occur. In an era where there is alarm that police tactics are overly aggressive or out of touch with community concerns, risk-based policing offers alternative ways of informing police decisions, targeting officer deployments, and engaging with community stakeholders (for mutual benefits) that leads to greater success in crime prevention compared to traditional practices. The need for transparency and accountability is intense at this juncture in policing. Civic leaders are calling for new tools and new insights to provide a new openness to policing practices. So, the willingness to move forward with risk-based policing exists among some key constituencies. But effectively adopting these new ideas and approaches requires local police leaders to be willing to ask new questions, collect new data, and find value in the empirical (but contextualized) results to aid in achieving public safety. Information and analysis must guide decisions about where to police, and also about what to do beyond law enforcement actions when resources get to particular places. Risk-based policing requires more than technological changes or software upgrades. It requires police leaders to adopt a mission that differentiates the practice of law enforcement from the promise of public safety and to deliver on both of these needs in coordinated and complementary fashion. People are not only seen in the equation as either potential victims or offenders to be guarded or captured but as stakeholders to partner with and learn from.

Risk-based policing responds to the demands of problem-oriented policing by offering a way to measure the contextual effects of environments on behavior and then establish how effective interventions are implemented to reduce the risk that may occur at these places. Risk-based policing is problem *solving,* not merely problem orientation. It offers an extension of the previous attempts at focused policing, discussed in chapter 2, that is evidence-based and actionable. Risk-based policing agencies that engage with community members to share information and solicit new insights on public safety further succeed at reducing the long-term risk of crime and its rate of occurrence. Members of the public who are directly or indirectly affected by crime problems engage with police as problem-solvers to promote processes and outcomes intended for the community. Public engagement enables evidence-based decision-making and increased transparency of policing while still keeping sensitive law enforcement information confidential or undisclosed. With all this in mind, and with a goal of crime prevention, the most effective risk-based policing leaders follow the central tenets in ways that are consistent with the goals of both public safety and law enforcement. They incorporate them into the three steps of risk-based policing, discussed in chapter 1. In the next chapter we will explore how risk-based policing relates to risk governance.

NOTES

1. An extensive review of the principles and techniques of RTM is presented in Caplan and Kennedy (2016) and can be explored through updated material on www.riskterrainmodeling.com.

2. In anticipating where displacement might occur, RTM provides a way of identifying and monitoring locations where crime incidents emerge. This process can be iterative, with a test/retest approach that allows for a shifting of treatment from one location to another as the crime patterns move. This allows for a flexible approach not possible when the emphasis is on territory clearly defined by the boundaries of existing crime hot spots.

3. Spatial influence serves as the measurable link between features of a landscape and their impacts on people and the ways they use space. Spatial vulnerability to crime will not change

unless one or more factors that comprise the risk terrain are mitigated. The secret, then, is that spatial vulnerabilities are mitigated by focusing efforts on reducing or eliminating spatial influences, and not necessarily just the risky features themselves. The effect of spatial influence is not a constant but one that can be altered to reduce risk. So, it is sensible to consider a risk reduction strategy that focuses on mitigating spatial influences. If the spatial influences of risky features increase the chance of crime and its patterns over time, then it should be equally the case that reducing these spatial influences would reduce the incidence of crime (Caplan and Kennedy 2016).

4

RISK-BASED POLICING AND ACTION

> **KEY POINTS**
>
> - Risk-based policing uses risk governance as a way of applying evidence-based practice to resource allocation and problem-solving.
> - Through risk-based policing, crime and other public safety risks become a responsibility shared by all.
> - ACTION meetings give multiple stakeholders objective information to exercise their intuition and foster greater confidence in decision-making for risk governance.

INTRODUCTION

Risk governance is the management of data, empirical analyses, uncertainties, and human judgments. Risk-based policing is risk governance focused on crime problems. Some police departments simply use software right out of the box to map risky places and then prioritize police patrols. With this basic strategy of risk governance, police are deployed to the most likely places for crime whereby their presence at the right place and times creates a deterrent effect. With RTM, these police patrols are constantly attuned to dynamic patterns and attractors of crime. Officers get useful instructions on what risky features to focus on at high-risk locations. Of course, mere police presence at risky places is not a cure for crime, because it does not mitigate the underlying attractors that drive criminal activity to these places. So, some police leaders take risk-based policing to the next level with ACTION meetings, which engage communities and coordinate crime prevention and risk reduction activities among multiple agencies and stakeholders.

RISK GOVERNANCE AND THE POLICE LEADER

We live in a "risk society" (Van Brunschot and Kennedy 2008), where crime and other threats to public safety have become a focus of agencies to control through selective application of resources (Beck 1992). Risk governance addresses the ways in which agencies plan for and react to these threats and incidents, in particular by the judgments they make about resource allocation. In this regard, risk governance is already highly valued in policing, whereby law enforcement resources are routinely geographically directed to affect crime rates. It is through risk-based policing that crime risk governance in police agencies becomes standardized and normalized. Actionable prescriptions from risk assessments are made to deploy resources to combat threats and their consequences, and law enforcement becomes integrated with community engagement. The emphasis on risk governance empowers police departments to share the burden of public safety with multiple stakeholders through data-driven evidence as justification for collaborative action.

Police agencies spearhead risk-based policing initiatives. Police monitor connections to crime, assess spatial vulnerabilities and exposures,[1] and prescribe actions to reduce the worst effects of these risk assessments. In so doing, they listen to both empirical evidence and subjective human judgment and blend the two. Police officers relate context to the data and communicate meaning out of the signals and noise of various information sources. The movement in policing toward risk governance reflects recognition that the threats facing communities go well beyond policing, personal victimizations, or crime-related harms, to include both real and perceived geopolitical, societal, economic, and political threats to a wide array of stakeholders (Martin and Mazerolle 2016). Through risk-based policing, crime and other public safety risks become a responsibility shared by all.

ACTION MEETINGS

Through the implementation of an ACTION agenda, police departments identify key stakeholders in the community to make them aware of policing efforts and to solicit their investments of time and expertise in risk reduction activities. Their insights improve the police department's understanding of the crime problem, thus helping further minimize uncertainty (an issue we will discuss later in this chapter). Effective police responses to crime problems vary dramatically across jurisdictions. Partly, this is determined by the local population's experiences with crime threats, but it is also a function of the degree of trust the public puts in police and their measured ability to successfully enhance public safety. Public confidence and commitment depend on the degree to which the public becomes a partner in risk governance, working with police agencies to deter crime and reduce risks. ACTION meetings facilitate this partnership among police and other stakeholders. The ACTION agenda focuses on Assessment, Connections, Tasks, Interventions, Outcomes, and Notifications.

Two groups of stakeholders, or task forces, are recommended for risk-based policing with ACTION: a police task force and a multi-stakeholder task force. The police task force is comprised of officers and other leaders of the police department spearheading the risk-based policing initiative. This includes the police leadership, commanding officers, certain patrol officers, detectives, and other law enforcement or security-related partners who operate within the jurisdiction and who can be privy to sensitive intelligence for law enforcement eyes only. The police task force meets regularly (e.g., monthly) to assess the RTM forecasts and to propose ways to govern crime risks from law enforcement and policing perspectives. For example, in one case using this approach, consensus was reached that three activities could be feasible and likely effective at priority high-risk places: (1) frequent directed patrols, with attention paid to the three risk factors (convenience stores, laundromats, and vacant properties) located at and around these places; (2) meet-and-greets at risky facilities (e.g., community policing), with sign-in sheets to be located with managers at these businesses to record the check-ins at frequent intervals during every shift; and (3) prioritizing these activities during peak time periods for crime.

The multi-stakeholder task force can be comprised of members of the police task force as well as city officials and other community leaders. This includes, but is not limited to, representatives from the mayor's office and various city departments, such as planning and development or public works; representatives of the mercantile associations, human and social service agencies, faith-based organizations, and local non-governmental organizations (e.g., neighborhood associations); school officials; business/store owners; and county and state executives. This multi-stakeholder task force opines on the risk-based policing initiatives from a broad public perspective and proposes risk governance activities that *they* can engage in to complement policing efforts. Meetings of the multi-stakeholder task force are not open, town-hall-style meetings where grievances get aired. They are by-invitation-only working meetings where risk assessments are shared and ground-truthed, data are managed, and initiatives to reduce risks are proposed and committed to by various stakeholders.

The leaders who spearhead the risk-based policing initiative in the police department should facilitate all task force meetings. The ACTION agenda, as outlined in figures 2 and 3, guides both the police and multi-stakeholder task force meetings, which is why they are called ACTION meetings. The next section of this chapter presents a more detailed discussion of the ACTION agenda items. ACTION meetings focus crime-risk-reduction activities on risky places and the known risk factors that can be addressed appropriately by all parties involved. ACTION meetings recur perpetually so that assessments, connections,

FIGURE 2
The ACTION agenda is applied iteratively
and consistently for risk-based policing.

Assessment of the risk narrative:
A spoken or written account of connected events.

Connections:
What attracts illegal behavior to high-crime areas and why crimes cluster there over time.

Task management:
Decide the feasibility of and responsibility for collecting data, performing analyses, and responding to information and spatial intelligence.

Intervention planning/implementation:
Present spatial analyses and develop interventions. Identify ways in which the problem occurs in the study setting, and the factors that are important in elevating risks of it continuing.

Outcome evaluation:
Measure changes in crime counts, spatial patterns of crime events, and risk values. Check for diffusion of benefits and displacement. Check whether proper procedures were implemented.

Notifying others:
Share information. Utilize technology, media outlets, and personal communications to share key information about risk reduction efforts with a variety of stakeholders.

FIGURE 3
Overview of the ACTION agenda.

tasks, interventions, outcome evaluations, and notifications can be updated, shared, and revised as the spatial and situational dynamics of crimes change over time. ACTION meetings enable ongoing reliability of decisions and responsive actions across task force groups. They give multiple stakeholders objective information to exercise their intuition and foster greater confidence in decision-making for risk governance.

A DETAILED BREAKDOWN OF THE ACTION AGENDA

ACTION begins with an *assessment* of the risk narrative as perceived by police or other stakeholders. They articulate how *they* understand the crime problem and related event contexts. Police leaders ask questions to gain insights that will ground their crime analysis methods in the nuanced social, cultural, economic, and political atmospheres in which the crime problem is happening. This grounded approach identifies potential threats to construct validity that could affect analyses and interpretations of results. It helps police analysts identify data sets and *connect* potential risk factors and their spatial influences to outcome events. And it begins the process of *task management,* whereby the police and other stakeholders discuss the feasibility and responsibilities of all parties to perform tasks to collect data and use risk assessments given known constraints and existing strengths of human capital and other resources. Then police analyze data and produce reports for *intervention planning.* RTM is a key component of ACTION at this point. RTM results are reviewed in ACTION meetings for various perspectives to interpret event contexts and the social relevancies of risk factors. Following the planning and implementation of intervention activities, police evaluate *outcomes* and *notify* everyone about what was done, why things were done, and the sustainability of efforts used to achieve positive results.

ASSESSMENT

As discussed in chapter 3, a risk narrative is a spoken or written account, or story, of how events, such as crimes, relate to other phenomena in the jurisdiction. Assessing the risk narrative is an endeavor to get police and other stakeholders thinking spatially about criminal events and behaviors. The goal in assessing the risk narrative is to identify patterns of behavior and understand how these behaviors engage with the environment and interact with other things to yield specific outcomes. Underlying the risk narrative is the basic premise that stakeholders engaged in this activity provide information that can be incorporated into risk governance—to promote proactive planning rather than reactive programs. Broadly speaking, an assessment of the risk narrative should characteristically seek to elucidate problems and issues that are high in relevance to the crime problem or related policies, practices, events and individuals. So, the steps would involve the following:

- What is the problem?
- Who is involved and/or affected by the problem?

- How do various stakeholders understand key issues and reconcile contested claims about the problem, its presumed causes, and/or what should be done to address it?
- What has already been done to address the problem?
- How should "success" be defined when future actions are taken to mitigate the problem?

CONNECTIONS

The task of making connections involves identifying factors that might spatially or temporally correlate with the crime problem, and valid and reliable data sets for measures thereof; developing new collection and management protocols for needed data sets; and distilling probable links between potential risk factors and their relationships to existing crime incidents. Connections emanate from the risk narrative. This is the stage where engaging with community stakeholders early on can yield mutual benefit and begin to establish the police agency's intentions for transparency in risk governance.

TASKS

A key goal of task management is to decide the responsibilities for performing tasks to collect data, perform analyses, and respond to information and risk assessments given known constraints and existing strengths of human capital and other resources. Task management considers who does what, with which resources, and when. Risk-based policing assumes that stakeholders (or their agencies) will not just collect information about crime problems but also, as part of risk governance, prescribe and supervise activities in which to address the risks. Task managers add accountability to this process.

INTERVENTIONS

As stated earlier, RTM results are used by police and other stakeholders to develop and implement actions for risk governance at high-risk places. The main purpose of an RTM report is to articulate the ways in which the problem under study occurs in the jurisdiction, the factors that are important in elevating the risks of it continuing, and where current vulnerabilities are located. The report provides guidance to decision-makers concerning what the analytical information means and how it relates to risk narratives. RTM reports offer insights for steps that can be taken to translate the data analysis into actionable intelligence for resource allocation and tactics to combat crime threats and their consequences. We have seen risk-based policing agencies refer to their custom versions of this report as an IPIR, or intervention planning intel report. The IPIR identifies target areas and prioritizes the risk factors to be addressed relative to their impact on the crime problem. This is done so that resources can be allocated and people can be told what to do about the places when they get there. The IPIR presents a structured evidence-based analysis using data. It is judged in the context of the combined insights of expert practitioners and other stakeholders to assess the spatial and temporal dynamics of the problem at hand. This permits informed decision-making during the planning and implementation stages of interventions.

With an IPIR in hand, conversations among police officials and other stakeholders (i.e., task force group members, via ACTION meetings) advance the risk narrative and ground-truth connections among several factors. They plan interventions and then formalize the management of tasks. For each risk factor identified in the risk terrain model, stakeholders are asked to explain how they understand its relationship to the crime problem. What are the likely mechanisms at play that link the risk factor to the crimes? After connections are made between factors in the risk terrain model and the crime problem, risk factors that should receive focused attention are prioritized. Police are encouraged to select some or all of the spatial risk factors whose effects they believe have the greatest potential for mitigation. Other stakeholders also conduct an honest assessment of their internal capacity and available resources in selecting risk factors for their own intervention activities. For example, foreclosures (distinct from abandoned properties) often appear as a significant risk factor in many cities. However, foreclosures are not usually directly addressed in policing intervention strategies, given the police department's belief that they are ill prepared to address the foreclosure crisis. However, a city planning department or a city's economic development committee may consider this risk factor within its domain. Once factors are selected to receive focused attention, the group proposes actions that police and other agencies can take to mitigate the risks and manage the consequences of known threats. Ultimately, these will be the activities that will occur as part of the newest iteration of risk reduction strategies under the risk-based policing initiative. Risk-based interventions generally include multiple activities related to mitigation of spatial influences of risk factors, situational crime prevention, directed police patrols, and enforcement activities (including municipal policies and regulations).

Selecting target areas for risk-based policing interventions is a straightforward evidence-based process that can adjust as needed to reflect a dynamic risk terrain and limited resources. High-risk places identified by RTM should be the target areas. High-risk places that intersect with recent crime hot spots can be further prioritized, as discussed in chapter 6. This helps prevent some areas from being under-resourced or over-policed, and it efficiently enhances strategic and tactical allocation of resources to places that need them most.

OUTCOMES

With a clearly articulated set of goals expressed for risk reduction strategies, the required data can be more easily defined and efforts made (i.e., through task management) to collect them. Outcome evaluations involve establishing whether or not the intervention that was implemented actually worked, meeting or exceeding expectations. Risk-based policing is not only interested in the state of the crime problem prior to the implementation of risk reduction strategies, but also concerned with the changes that can be attributed to the activities happening in the targeted areas. There is an extensive literature in many fields on the steps that are needed to evaluate the success or failure of intervention activities. The most popular measure of success is a crime-rate drop. The simple desistance of crime must be supported, however, through systematic observation and careful documentation of changes, whether they are increases or decreases in criminal activity. This enables assigning credit to effective activities and improving on those that did not meet expectations.

In addition to a measure of crime counts, outcome evaluations should assess changes in the spatial patterns of crime-incident locations. Outcomes can also include diffusion of benefits and assessment of whether crime displacement occurred (e.g., to high-risk places elsewhere in the jurisdiction). Police have also been able to measure their influence on mitigating the spatial influences of risky features by assessing changes in a targeted risk factor's "relative risk value" in post-intervention risk terrain models. Regularly updated risk terrain models assess these changing spatial patterns in offender preferences. Outcome evaluations are needed so task force members can, in turn, readjust with fresh intelligence products and intervention strategies. This allows police to anticipate crime displacement and stay ahead of emerging problems. Risk-based policing can also lead to new approaches to measuring police productivity that go beyond a heavy reliance on traditional law enforcement practices. This is apropos of the current demand of police departments by the constituents they serve to demonstrate effectiveness without increasing arrest statistics (Sparrow 2015). Within six months of risk-based policing in Atlantic City, the police department was credited with a 20% reduction in violent crimes; the need for arrests decreased, community relations improved, and cost savings to the local criminal justice system amounted to nearly $300,000 (McCollister, French, and Feng 2010).

Whereas outcome evaluations assess the effectiveness of an intervention in producing an intended change, process evaluations can help the task force see how an intervention outcome was achieved (i.e., for better or worse) and then improved upon. Process evaluations look at the different roles that key actors played and their effectiveness in meeting intervention objectives. Included in this review could be a survey of participants or, more simply, an open discussion with task managers about their role in the initiatives; how they believed the work that they or their agencies did impacted on intended goals; and suggestions for improved and more effective risk-management resources. It is important to give feedback to all stakeholders involved in risk-based policing so they can see transparency in repeated iterations of the program.

NOTIFICATIONS

Notifying others involves communicating information. An RTM report notifies task force members about risk assessments. But notification in ACTION requires more. It should utilize technology, media outlets, and personal communications to share key information about risk-based policing efforts with a variety of stakeholder populations. It should open interactions between civilian and sworn personnel; analysts and officers; police and other municipal departments; elected officials and constituents; and public and private entities. We have witnessed that when police take initiatives to contact residents about crime risk, the public responds positively. We have also documented how police agencies focused on risk governance consider themselves a resource for the community that is intended to reduce their vulnerability to crime—that is, where the identification of risky places does not necessarily demand an allocation of increased law enforcement but, rather, an increased need for community resources. Allocation of resources is not something that police departments do in isolation. We have seen this in cities like Edmonton, Alberta, Canada, where Stephane Contre and Kris Andreychuk solicited partnerships in risk governance by leveraging RTM to assess precipitating contextual factors that are correlated with crime. Then they thoughtfully responded with a variety of city resources before chronic problems emerge. The city of Edmonton has revealed narratives for crime that call into question preconceived notions and related biases and present various city agencies new opportunities for coordinated problem-solving with a shared goal of public safety.

Notifying others is heavily intertwined with public relations. The Fayetteville, NC, Police Department incorporated risk-based policing into the Community Wellness Plan in 2013, which was briefed by the police chief to the city council at its January meeting. Then in 2016, Captain Nolette wrote an essay, published in the National Institute of Justice's journal, about how the department was using research to move policing forward. The department also presented on its efforts at the annual meeting of the International Association of Crime Analysts. They actively sought out multiple audiences to notify about their efforts. Risk-based policing should be a transparent evidence-based approach to managing crime risks in ways that are tailored to specific real and perceived threats that affect people living in the jurisdiction. Notifications about risk governance can have a substantial positive effect on public safety and should be one of the people-oriented aspects of risk-based policing. Having clearly informed decisions and risk narratives that back up responses to crime risks goes a long way to provide context in which police officers, elected officials, the media, and the general public can judge the likelihood of successful outcomes and prospects for the problems faced in communities. Notifying others (via a variety of media) about risk-based policing efforts, including being honest (and humble) about outcomes, facilitates community stakeholder relationships and increases the potential for long-term success with risk governance.

THE UNCERTAINTY IN RISK GOVERNANCE

Uncertainty is part of decision-making. According to renowned psychologists Amos Tversky and Daniel Kahneman, the job of decision-makers is not to be right every time but to figure out the odds in any decision they have to make and play the odds well (Lewis

2016, 248). This is not easy or natural for most people (including the authors of this book!). In 1953 the French economist Maurice Allais offered an example of these aspects of human nature, which has since been called the Allais paradox. He asked his audience to make decisions about what to do in two situations (as cited in Lewis 2016, 259). The choices that most people made were perfectly sensible, but also complete contradictions of mathematical logic. Ultimately, public safety depends on how well policy-makers and practitioners assess the odds, or the risks, of crime threats before making decisions about mitigation and response. The odds of achieving accurate crime predictions matter greatly for target-area selection and resource allocation, and these can be improved through multimodal analysis methods. Beyond predictions, considerations of risk pressure decision-makers to anticipate the future and to minimize uncertainty while planning for, preventing, or managing the negative effects of what is likely to occur at particular places.

Risk assessment is the consideration of the probabilities of particular outcomes (Kennedy and van Brunschot 2009). Risk is probabilistic, so the extent to which police can minimize uncertainty influences how well they are able to judge crime threats and their consequences. "Wherever there is uncertainty there has got to be judgment," explained Don Redelmeier, a medical internist at Canada's Sunnybrook Hospital whose job it was to check the understanding of medical specialists for mental errors (Lewis 2016). The complexity of such uncertainty is further contextualized by Lewis, who argued that "wherever there is judgment there is an opportunity for human fallibility" (213–14). Realizing what we do not know helps determine the confidence level for what we do know. At some point, even the most data-driven, artificially intelligent predictions must invite human judgment into the decision-making processes. In fact, this is built into risk-based policing by way of risk narratives and the ACTION agenda. Crime risk assessment is that moment where predictive analytics is considered in the context of various other pieces of information so that judgments can be made about managing crime risks with the greatest odds of short- and long-term success.

Shortly after an off-duty police officer was shot and killed in 2011 in Newark, NJ, while waiting in line to buy pizza, city council members voted unanimously to approve an ordinance requiring restaurants in "high-crime areas" to close their doors at 10 P.M. on weekdays and 11 P.M. on Fridays and Saturdays (Giambusso 2012). A list of streets throughout the city that were thought to be problematic according to city council members' insights was compiled. Ultimately, 17 neighborhoods throughout Newark were affected by the ordinance. The ordinance was endorsed by the police director, who cited a perceived difference between urban and suburban communities in the relation between crime rates and hours of operation of take-out restaurants. Other perceptions led city officials to understand violent behaviors near "chicken shacks" and pizza joints to be interrelated after Officer Johnson was killed waiting in line at a business named Texas Fried Chicken and Pizza. One city council member explained that these take-out restaurants that stay open late do little to serve the community and encourage crime. This relationship seemed obvious to many elected officials, and so, too, was the enacted treat-

FIGURE 4
Which line is longer?

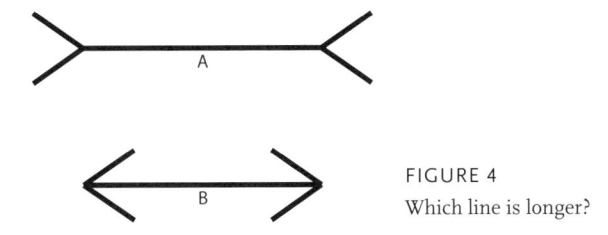

ment. But the observations and related treatment may have failed to account for unknowns, such as alternative facilities or places with similar criminogenic qualities. Ultimately, no outcome evaluations were conducted to learn about the true impact of the legislative response.

In another U.S. municipality, city officials responded to a nighttime spike in violent crimes by enacting an ordinance requiring convenience stores to close at 10 P.M. The observed relationship between convenience stores and crime appeared obvious to many key decision-makers, and so the political and legislative response made intuitive sense. But the new law ultimately failed to mitigate the situational contexts of these events and increased the risk of violent crimes at similar environments elsewhere in the city. After 10 P.M., crimes emerged around gas stations with food marts, which were exempted from the city ordinance. At these gas stations, certain environmental qualities generated suitable new contexts for violence to emerge.

In both of these all-too-common scenarios, reasonable human perceptions led to potentially faulty policy judgments. There were no data-driven efforts to test perceptions or to reliably reduce uncertainty prior to the decision about treatments being made. Consider one of the most famous optical illusions, named after Franz Carl Müller-Lyer, a German sociologist, who created it in 1889. In figure 4, which line is longer?

Presented with these two lines of equal length, the eye is tricked into seeing one as longer than the other. Even after it is proven to people, with a ruler, that the lines are identical lengths, the illusion persists. If perception has the power to overwhelm reality in such a simple case (Lewis 2016, 78), how susceptible to failure might the critically unchecked judgments of many smart and experienced public safety officials be? An American psychologist named Edward Thorndike suggested that even a very capable professional is unable to view a problem or issue as a compound of separate qualities and to assign a magnitude to each of these in independence of the others (Lewis 2016, 79).

Public safety officials are challenged by the lack of complete and accurate data on all relevant factors of crime events or motivated offenders and the potential for misperceptions of threats and priorities. One of the key steps to addressing this is to acknowledge the innate limitations of even experienced human intuitions and professional observations because of uncertainties that exist in decision-making processes. In such a context of uncertainty, a goal of risk-based policing is to reduce "egregious errors" in risk assessments. This is done through synthesizing information derived from human judgments, data, and empirical analyses in the context of known uncertainties, and bringing this into decision-making regarding actions focused on crime prevention and risk reduction. This is risk-based policing with RTM and ACTION.

CONCLUSION

Police agencies that did not previously discuss their work in terms of risk are now using risk-based policing to guide their planning and operations. This is true in local law enforcement as much as it is becoming common in state and federal agencies and the corporate sector. Private businesses seek to ensure that the risk-management mission is instituted enterprise-wide and provides communication channels to decision-makers for asset protection and security threats (Marsh and Noonan 2005, 4). In addition to responding to probabilistic modeling of crime vulnerabilities and exposures, risk-based policing seeks to establish police management practices that optimize prevention, response, and mitigation of crimes and crime risks. This works best when police leaders establish buy-in at all levels of the police agency.

Guided by ACTION, risk-based policing uses data-driven judgments to reduce uncertainty in the mission of crime risk governance for the goal of sustainable public safety. Risk-based policing extends the strong tradition of geographic analysis in the policing profession, and takes advantage of contemporary analytical and technical tools like RTM within the ACTION agenda to improve and extend this history. What risk-based policing demonstrates is that police leaders can tell patrol officers where to go to confront crime but also, based on their understanding of spatial vulnerabilities and exposures, what to do when they get there, and how they can get other stakeholders engaged in the process. With growing societal expectations that police should single-handedly respond to crime problems, police leaders are realizing that the burden of public safety needs to be shared to manage crime threats before incidents emerge or cluster. Risk-based policing with RTM and ACTION is the modality that empowers police to prevent crime and assign shared responsibility for public safety.

RTM aids in the task of determining threats in an environment and marshaling resources to moderate the worst effects. But to efficiently and effectively act on risk assessments, police agencies must also enlist the support of a variety of other stakeholders. Risk-based policing with RTM and ACTION empowers police to solicit resources and support in articulable and convincing ways. Members of the public who are directly or indirectly affected by crime problems and solicited for this purpose can include representatives from a number of different constituencies. Leaders in the police department can engage with them at ACTION meetings as potential problem-solvers to promote investment by the community in the process and outcomes intended for the community. Such public engagement enables less siloed decision-making and more transparency of policing. The result is sustainable crime risk governance, measurable crime reductions, and enhanced public safety throughout the jurisdiction.

GETTING STARTED

The key to risk-based policing is to just start doing it. Establish a test period, or pilot project, to set expectations. Identify key data sets. Forge buy-in. Start making risk terrain models for an acute problem such as robberies, burglaries, drug overdoses, or vehicle crashes. Get a feel for RTM using data that are readily available to you. Review the results and practice designing risk reduction strategies informed by the RTM outputs. Try tabletop exercises with a small group of people in your agency. Then try an ACTION meeting. Once you get started, you will quickly realize that RTM informs key decisions inherent in policing and risk governance. Once you are comfortable with the technical aspects, establish a process for repeated iterations of spatial risk assessment, resource deployment, and data collection to check for success. In short order these steps of risk-based policing will become the standard procedure for policing in your jurisdiction.

Some police departments simply use RTM software (RTMDx) to quickly map risky places and prioritize police patrols. Other agencies take risk-based policing to the next level with police-only ACTION meetings, and then, in due time, multi-stakeholder ACTION meetings are added to the lineup to engage communities and coordinate crime prevention and risk reduction activities among multiple people and agencies. Where to begin is up to you.

NOTE

1. We will discuss exposure and vulnerability when we introduce the theory of risky places in part 2.

PART 2

METHODS AND CASE STUDIES OF RISK-BASED POLICING

Having introduced risk-based policing, it is time to turn to theoretical concepts and methodological best practices to demonstrate its efficacy and effectiveness through scientific experiments already completed. Risk-based policing has benefited from extensive support from the U.S. Department of Justice in funding partnerships that have launched risk-based policing initiatives in cities across the United States. Our collaborations with police agencies have shown the merit of risk-based policing, and other researchers have taken it on themselves to test it as well, relying on tools that we have provided through webinars and workshops that offer extensive resources for developing their initiatives. We will discuss some of these projects here, explaining how they were conceived, the major steps involved in managing the implementations that were part of these initiatives, and our assessment of the benefits and challenges of these efforts.

5

THE THEORY OF RISKY PLACES

> **KEY POINTS**
> - Risk-based policing uses the theory of risky places to identify locations where environmental factors interact to raise vulnerability and exposure to crime.
> - The crime risk kaleidoscope characterizes the combination of risk factors and the process whereby they represent the formation of behavior settings in one environment or another.
> - The aggregate neighborhood risk of crime measure simultaneously accounts for characteristics of the built environment and social factors known to be robust correlates of levels of crime and violence at macro social units of analysis.

INTRODUCTION

In this chapter we explain how risk-based policing relates to the literature on criminology, crime analysis, and policing. Through the application of risk terrain modeling (RTM) within the ACTION agenda, risk-based policing assesses risk in physical environments and operationalizes it for governance by police and other stakeholders in practical ways. This risk governance is predicated on existing criminological theories and methods. In particular, risk-based policing is grounded in decades of research evidence. It is the embodiment of the theory of risky places. Risk-based policing enables the use of information that comes from non-traditional police administrative records, such as complaints about poor services or the proliferation of graffiti or abandoned buildings. It even permits investigations of how risky locations are defined by social disadvantage, low collective efficacy, physical decay, neglect or abandonment. In so doing, risk-based policing enables evaluation of the efficacy of broken windows theory, social disorganization theory, ecological theory, social area analysis, and crime prevention through environmental design via an iterative process of assessing change in outcomes as a consequence of decisions to alter the design or qualities of certain risky places. Risk-based policing shifts the focus from theories and concepts of crime *opportunity* to theories and concepts of crime *risk*, which is far more calculable a priori.

THEORIES RELEVANT TO RISK-BASED POLICING

The theory of risky places proposes that risk levels of crime can and should be computed at places according to the interaction effects of known locational features. Risky places are particular portions of space that have been assessed for their likelihood of experiencing crimes and to which a relative risk value has been attributed. According to the theory, risky places are a product of the combined effects of vulnerabilities and exposures to crime, two concepts we introduced earlier in this book. Vulnerability comes from the presence of a combination of spatial influences of features of a landscape that enhance the likelihood of crime. This is articulated through RTM. Exposures are the historical facts and collective memories people have about places and the events that occurred there, such as knowledge about crime hot spots. A vulnerability–exposure analytical framework considers the integration of RTM *and* measures of exposures to crime, such as kernel density estimated (KDE) hot spots. This provides a basis for analyzing the system processes whereby crimes emerge, persist or disappear. The combined effects of vulnerability and exposure lead to the identification of risky places discussed later in this chapter (Caplan and Kennedy 2016).[1]

PLACE-BASED APPROACHES TO CRIME PREVENTION

Place-based crime prevention is an outgrowth of the environmental criminology movement, which heavily influenced both academia and professional practice beginning in the last quarter of the twentieth century and continues well into the present day. Environmental criminology represents a family of theories concerned with criminal events and the immediate circumstances in which they occur (Sacco and Kennedy 2002; Wortley and Mazerolle 2008). These include routine activities (Cohen and Felson 1979), rational choice (Clarke and Cornish 1985), and crime pattern theory (Brantingham and Brantingham 2008). Crime pattern theory is typically credited with connecting the tenets of routine activities and rational choice, explicitly operationalizing them to space (Andresen 2014, 8). Crime pattern theory considers daily behavior patterns as involving three activity spaces: nodes (places where people spend extended amounts of time, such as home, work, and places of recreation); paths (travel routes between nodes); and edges (boundaries between different areas). Activity spaces can be made criminogenic by the presence of crime generators and crime attractors, that is, features of the environment that enable crime through the attraction of large numbers of people and/or distinct criminal opportunities that are well known to offenders (Clarke and Eck 2005, 17).

Environmental criminology contends that places matter and that the built environment plays a pivotal role in where illegal behaviors resulting in crimes occur. Generally speaking, offenders and other people participate in activities that require them to move through an environment on a daily basis. As Cohen and Felson (1979, 595) pointed out, "the risk of criminal victimization varies dramatically among the circumstances and locations in which people place themselves and their property." This ecological distribution of crime opportunities is (perhaps) why Cohen, Kluegel, and Land (1981) refashioned routine activities theory to become "opportunity theory," which includes concepts of exposure, proximity, guardianship, and target attractiveness as variables that increase the risk of victimization.

The decision to act on criminal opportunities once the elements that increase the likelihood of victimization converge rests on the offender making a decision that crime, and its potential rewards, outweigh the risks (i.e., potentially getting caught/arrested). Presumably, rational offenders make this decision based on the limited information presented at the time of the criminogenic opportunity (Cornish and Clarke 1986). But environmental psychology suggests that situationally induced emotions can provoke a criminal response among both rational or irrational people.[2] If people commit illegal behavior enough in the same setting, the physical environment (itself) can shape the subsequent human behavior (even unconsciously). Psychologists refer to this as "outsourcing" control of behavior to the physical environment (Spiegel 2015). In a meta-analysis of police intervention programs, Braga, Papachristos, and Hureau (2012) report that decreases in crime relate not only to the offender-centric strategies but also to steps taken to modify the environments in which they operate. This finding complements criminological and psychological research that reveals how environments consciously or unconsciously influence behavior, and how efforts to reliably and accurately predict illegal behaviors based on environmental contexts are viable and important avenues for problem-solving and intervention planning (Louiselli and Cameron 1998; Kennedy and Forde 1998).

Risk-based policing focuses on risk, not opportunity, because risk is calculable based on a metric of what factors appear in the environment that connect to the crime being studied. Opportunity theory (Andresen 2014) tends to focus on the aggregate or macro level, contending that the more offenders discover opportunity, the more likely they are to act on it. Opportunities tie to rational choice, where, in the absence of a guardian or some other deterrent force, crime is seen as inevitable. This is not true most of the time. Nonetheless, policing and crime prevention based on opportunity theory depend on removing opportunities. While this is helpful in identifying how criminal offending might occur, the identification of a crime opportunity is not always clear before the event takes place. We can, of course, make a judgment about this after the fact and act accordingly in anticipation of the next occurrence. But even this post hoc assessment provides a dichotomous choice for analysts between crime or no crime. This thus reduces our ability to anticipate the likelihood of the offender or other similar offenders acting based on their own unique perceptions, at any given place and moment in time.

Crime pattern theory (Brantingham and Brantingham 2008) suggests that as people spend time within activity spaces, they develop a greater awareness of the space they occupy. For offenders, awareness space provides cues to the present (and other potentially suitable) environments where they feel free to commit crime. Characteristics of the physical environment that affect criminal opportunities at and around activity spaces are referred to as crime generators and attractors (Brantingham and Brantingham 2008). There is a large literature to show the wide variety of crime generators and attractors, such as parks, liquor stores, bars, and fast-food restaurants, that influence criminal behavior and crime locations. But assessment of vulnerable places must also account for the importance of the human factor, shifting the focus away from personal characteristics to personal preferences. Behavioral outcomes emerge as a function of dynamic interactions among people that occur at specific places. Attributes of places and the ways in which these attributes combine reveal consistent patterns of interaction. By adding the concept of risk to the picture, we are actually incorporating the judgment about choice directly into the incident itself. Risk is something that can be assigned to a situation based on the context in which a crime is about to occur. So, while it may be the case that a bar offers an opportunity for crime, its presence also raises the risk that a crime will occur at places nearby. Added to this risk assessment can be other factors that are computed to examine cumulative risk. Addressing these risks can have the effect of reducing opportunities, but can be done in a way that addresses contextual precursors as well as the actual exposure that comes from offenders taking advantage of circumstances.

Risk-based policing focuses not only on the risk itself, but also on the relationships of these risks to crime outcomes in discernable patterns throughout the landscape. Crime pattern theory assumes that there are distinct ways in which crimes cluster, partly as a result of previous crime occurrence, but also because of the distinctive characteristics of the environment in which it occurs. While it is important to understand how each of the factors in the environment is conducive to crime, it is also necessary to identify relationships that exist between these features. In a paper we authored with Jeremy Barnum (Barnum et al. 2017), we explain how context can be understood based on the basic principles of crime pattern theory, demonstrating that the configurations of these spatial effects could vary from jurisdiction to jurisdiction. We argued that place features that generate and attract crime are distributed throughout the landscape along various paths,

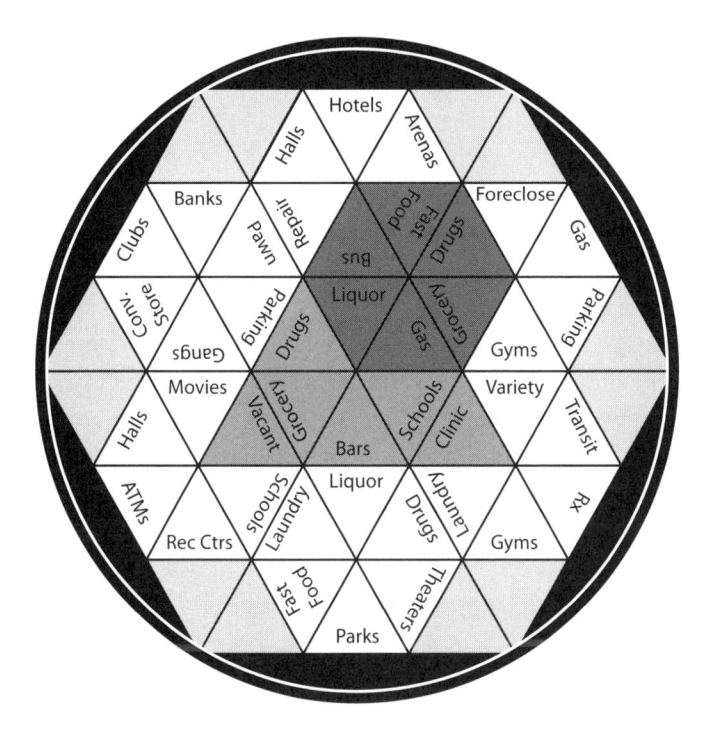

FIGURE 5
The crime risk kaleidoscope.

or the routes people take (e.g., roads, sidewalks, etc.). They also follow edges, or distinct changes in the landscape (e.g., railways, changes in land use, neighborhood boundaries, etc.), which create nodes, or areas of intense activity (Brantingham and Brantingham 1985). However, the distribution of these features throughout each jurisdiction's environmental backcloth is unique, the result of various processes involving local policies and regulations with regard to zoning, infrastructure, and urban planning. Physical landscapes are constructed around natural terrains and molded around particular social, cultural, historical, and economic systems, all of which influence their unique form and function and ongoing changes and developments. The combination of these forces ensures distinctiveness in the image of cities and the ways in which behavior in them unfolds (Lynch 1960).

Kennedy (1983, 11) conceptualizes this through the analogy of a kaleidoscope (figure 5). The kaleidoscope represents an environment (e.g., city A), and the shards of glass embody place features (e.g., bars, restaurants, public transportation stops) in that environment. The arrangement of place features encompasses an environment's form. Moving from one environment to the next (e.g., from city A to city B), or turning the kaleidoscope, alters the form of that environment. Central to the analogy is that the patterning of features varies between environments, but the parts and processes that create these patterns are the same. Thus, it is the particular combinations of features at places in different environments that must be identified to understand the distribution of behaviors, including criminal offending.

Early ecological research demonstrated that crime is more likely in some areas of a city compared to others and suggested that there is value in considering what it is about those areas, beyond the individuals that exist there, that fosters illegal behavior. However, the ecologists primarily focused on community social and demographic characteristics and largely neglected the influence of the physical features of environments on crime. Modern advances in data and technology have allowed researchers to demonstrate that crime is highly concentrated at very specific places. In this regard, several environmental criminology perspectives have emerged to provide a theoretical basis to this phenomenon. These perspectives discuss how physical place features throughout the environmental backcloth can generate or attract crime by structuring the everyday routines of individuals and creating good opportunities for offending. Each jurisdiction has a unique backcloth, and the particular ways in which certain features come together to create conditions for illegal behavior may not generalize, even for the same type of crime. Therefore, it is important to identify these patterns within the environmental backcloth of each jurisdiction to understand the more localized spatial dynamics of crime. RTM does this and permits risk-based policing initiatives to operationalize and measure local environmental backcloths in such a way. The advantage of risk-based policing with RTM is that we can take account of the co-location of risk factors. This allows us to examine the spatial influence of each factor separately, in terms of proximity and concentration effects, and the cumulative effects of these factors together to form higher-risk places.

Human ecologists were particularly interested in the ways in which urban form was created through the impact of competition between ethnic groups, different family types, and locations defined by economic status (Burgess and Park 1921). The modeling they performed suggested that there would be standardized changes to the urban fabric based on this competition and it would form locations in which groups would congregate. By improving on the ecological approach, a risk-based approach enables a micro-level analysis of component risk factors not possible in previous methods. In particular, risk-based policing with RTM provides a way of testing the impact of crime prevention through an iterative process of assessing change in outcomes as a consequence of decisions to alter the contexts of certain environments.

ENVIRONMENTS AND CRIME PREVENTION

You might ask, "What, specifically, about environments should be altered in high-crime areas?" This question brings to mind police and other stakeholders' efforts at crime prevention through environmental design (CPTED; Cozens and Love 2015). Altering the physical design of communities in which humans reside and congregate is a main goal of CPTED. However, CPTED without RTM is like playing darts blindfolded (and not even knowing whether you are in the same room as the target before you throw). Risk reduction strategies informed by RTM can accommodate the ideas of CPTED in targeting certain locations for intervention, but they extend beyond situational crime prevention and opportunities for crime or a "crime triangle," and, instead, target all aspects of the context that raises the risk that crime will occur. The crime triangle refers to three presumed components of crime problems: presence of offenders, suitable targets, and lack of capable guardians. RTM provides risk-based policing with an approach to understanding crime occurrence that identifies the relative influences of environmental factors that contribute to crime and behavior. Risk terrain maps inform decisions about which places can be targeted to reduce these risks.

With its focus on environmental risks and efforts to mitigate spatial contexts for crime and disorder, risk-based policing also offers a way of evaluating broken windows theory, which suggests that decline in orderly behavior in certain physical locations leads to an escalation of crime problems through an operationalization of the key factors of the physical and social environment that might contribute to this link. Broken windows theory focuses on social disorder, but not in the ways previous ecological researchers did (Wilson and Kelling 1982). Instead of suggesting that physical decline creates conditions that are conducive to crime, the theory proposes a direct link between disorderly conduct (involving minor infractions) which occurs in these locations and serious crime. The solution to break this link, they argued, is to crack down on the less serious offenses as a way to curtail violent crime. This theory has been widely adopted in police circles but has taken on new controversy as over-aggressive policing tactics associated with it are seen as part of the reason for poor police–community relations, particularly in minority neighborhoods.

Broken windows–style police responses to crime have traditionally been offender-focused and, thus, disconnected from the ecological theories and spatial analyses that inform the response. Risk-based policing, instead, puts an emphasis on intervention activities that focus on places, not only people located at certain places. In an hour-long interview,[3] then New York City Police Commissioner Bill Bratton explained that the latest manifestation of frayed relations between the police and Black communities was a byproduct of the operationalization of broken windows theory, whereby lower-level offenses were given higher priority and police officers were mandated to measure productivity and demonstrate success on the job by stopping, frisking, citing, and arresting individuals in spatially defined problem areas. Ultimately, minority communities bore the brunt of this focused attention from police. Broken windows policing has been applied too extensively for many decades as a crime prevention strategy, all while being too disconnected from the root spatial causes of crime. It has become obvious that simmering frustrations and frayed relations between police and the public they serve can be exacerbated when crime analyses and intelligence products fail to elucidate root attractors of illegal behavior; especially when responses to spatial intelligence fail to address the qualities of places and fail to look beyond merely the people located there.

Risk-based policing provides a way of identifying and operationalizing the parts of crime-event contexts. But beyond that, it assists in recognizing patterns that appear in the landscape, accounting for spatial relationships and patterns through maps that identify change over time. In considering risk factors, risk-based policing aims to disrupt key spatial and situational contexts for crime through planned changes to the environment.

SOCIAL DISORGANIZATION

Risk-based policing can further incorporate assessments of physical decay, such as by including information on neglect, abandonment, and physical decline, to test social disorganization theory. A key assertion of the social disorganization approach is that the forces of physical decay, abandonment, and neglect all have an impact on crime (Bursik 1988); they promote social breakdown and are influential epicenters of crime. The tests for these types of relationships have conventionally looked at single-factor solutions (e.g. the effects of bus stops on crime) or relied on analysis that focuses on certain stereotyped locations, such as low-income neighborhoods, public housing, or areas that contain drug markets and gangs. While such research has been important in defining where crime might occur, as well as some of the principal reasons for this, it has tended to be disjointed and lacking consistent measures of analysis that would allow comparisons of how different aspects of disorganization combine to cause crime. Notable exceptions to this trend are the research programs that have looked at communities using systematic social observation techniques to establish qualitative benchmarks for analysis (Sampson and Raudenbush 1999). This early work has offered important insights into the effects of environmental degradation on crime, but it has been difficult to replicate and to standardize the measures that are used to identify disorder.

More recently, Grant Drawve and colleagues (Drawve, Thomas, and Walker 2016) incorporated neighborhood-disorganization and socioeconomic-disadvantage measures into risk analysis in an effort to better understand neighborhood-level crime risk. They used RTM to develop an aggregate neighborhood risk of crime (ANROC) measure, which simultaneously accounts for characteristics of the built environment and social factors known to be robust correlates of levels of crime and violence at macro social units of analysis. The ANROC study focused on Little Rock, Arkansas, which, according to Uniform Crime Reports, had the seventh-highest violent crime rate of cities in the United States with more than 100,000 residents in 2013. As in all cities, however, crime is not evenly or randomly dispersed across Little Rock neighborhoods. So the goal of Drawve and his colleagues was to explore the ability of neighborhood physical and social characteristics to assist in the prediction of variation in crime across neighborhoods. First, they used RTM to construct a spatial risk assessment for 2013 violent crime across the city. Similar to prior studies and applications of RTM, they found that violent crimes occurred most often in higher-risk places (at the micro level). Then, they aggregated the micro-level RTM risk scores to census tracts to calculate the ANROC. Higher-ANROC tracts were positively associated with violent crime rates. Finally, they tested ANROC while accounting for a concentrated socioeconomic disadvantage index and residential stability, previously well-known correlates of violent crime. Data for these social measures were obtained from the American Community Survey (2009–2013 five-year estimates). The measure of concentrated socioeconomic disadvantage was a summary index comprised of the average of six standardized items: median income (inverse), percentage unemployed, percentage of households in poverty, percentage of households receiving public assistance (food stamps/SNAP), percentage of residents who are African American, and percentage of households headed by a single female with children. A summary measure capturing neighborhood levels of residential stability was also used. The stability index was constructed through a principal component analysis that included the percentage of households that were owner-occupied and those in which residents have been in the community for at least a year. Findings revealed that simultaneously considering both the social and physical environments allowed a more complete understanding of variation in crime across places. In fact, the ANROC measure, the concentrated disadvantage index, and the residential stability index, when combined into a single model, account for significant effects on violence and explain 55% of the variation in neighborhood crime rates.

Clearly, both the physical environment and social structure play important roles in the occurrence, frequency, and distribution of crime by differentially exposing individuals to conditions conducive for offending and victimization. This lends itself well to risk-based policing in that risk terrains are not the only analytical products necessary for crime risk governance. Knowledge of situational and community contexts is needed for effective and long-term risk-mitigation efforts. This is why such insights are called for in the ACTION agenda. In most of the research that has been done to date, there are clearly established links between the social condition of municipal locations and crime, often as a consequence of the limited ability of residents to mobilize their own or public resources to protect them. They live, as a result, in areas of high insecurity. Attracted to these locations are individuals who take advantage of this vulnerability. The police role is to reduce the negative consequences of this high risk of crime on the affected communities, in particular, and the municipality at large. Risk-based policing offers a way of examining such relationships by identifying locations in terms of their specific risk profiles, based on measures that are place-based, as discussed above, and then analyzing their impact in the context of social disadvantage, through techniques such as RTM or ANROC. Risk-based policing allows the analysts, policy-makers, and practitioners to more closely tie crime-event contexts to the measurable levels of social disadvantage and to consider how these contexts might be in need of resources from a risk governance point of view.

Risk-based policing provides the means by which theoretically grounded interventions become a central part of the institutional activities of cities, generally, and police departments, specifically. It offers a means of determining the difference the resources directed at certain locations actually make over time in mitigating the observed and expected negative effects of social disorganization. It can be used to evaluate the extent to which efforts need to be sustained, expanded, or contracted as interventions are instituted over time.

CONCLUSION

Risk-based policing is firmly grounded in criminological theory and supported by extensive research. Most importantly, it incorporates elements of many different theories, allowing the most important and efficacious explanations and principles from the literature to be applied to professional practices in an evidence-based manner. The insights provided by the analysis products from the tests of the theory of risky places, the crime risk kaleidoscope, and ANROC broaden the applicability and efficacy of this approach as a place-based strategy for crime reduction and prevention.

The support that we derive from academic work promotes an ongoing partnership between researchers and practitioners, akin to the new ideas that have emerged around translational criminology (Kennedy, Irvin-Erikson, and Kennedy 2014). As these partnerships build, the results will be more transparent and effective for policing practices, and will further encourage multiple stakeholder involvement to effect public safety.

NOTES

1. Caplan and Kennedy (2016) demonstrate the value of this approach and the extent to which it facilitates targeting places for crime intervention. It is worth reviewing for those interested in the technical and theoretical details.

2. Environmental psychology is concerned with the effects of the natural and built environment on human behavior.

3. On Charlie Rose, aired January 12, 2015 (retrieved January 19, 2015, from http://www.hulu.com/watch/737448).

6

HIGH-RISK TARGET AREAS AND PRIORITY PLACES

> **KEY POINTS**
> - Spatial vulnerability to crime is assessed by risk terrain modeling to diagnose features of the environment that contribute to the emergence and persistence of crime hot spots.
> - High-risk places are forecast to experience the most crime, so they are the targets of police patrols and intervention activities.
> - Target areas are further prioritized based on the vulnerability–exposure framework that is grounded in the theory of risky places.
> - High-risk places that intersect with recent-past crime hot spots receive priority attention for risk-based policing.

INTRODUCTION

The subject of this chapter is identifying and selecting target areas for police deployments and risk reduction strategies. The efficacy of risk reduction efforts is maximized by selecting the micro-places most prone to, or at risk of, future crime occurrence. Our research on this key task of target-area selection for risk-based policing led us to a scientific approach that examines the effects of vulnerability and exposure on the occurrence of crime incidents. With its diagnosis of the environmental attractors of illegal behaviors, RTM makes very accurate forecasts of new crime locations. Forecasted high-risk areas become target areas for risk-based policing. The top 5 percent of highest-risk places have excellent predictive accuracy. But further prioritization of these places can allow more efficient deployments of limited resources, such as police patrols, and intervention activities that address the riskiest places first. Following exploratory testing with our colleague Grant Drawve using Project Safe Neighborhoods data from Jersey City, NJ, we recommend a vulnerability–exposure approach to target-area selection and prioritization that leverages two spatial-analysis techniques to evaluate crime patterns: RTM and kernel density estimation (KDE). So, risk-based policing should focus on high-risk areas identified through RTM. And, to further prioritize risk reduction efforts, immediate priority should be given to the high-risk areas that intersect with recent-crime hot spots.

STUDYING EXPOSURE AND VULNERABILITY TO CRIME

Exposure to crime is often assessed with hot spot mapping. This computation includes techniques such as KDE (Chainey, Thompson, and Uhlig 2008), spatial and temporal analysis of crime (Block and Block 2004), or nearest neighborhood hierarchical clustering (Levine 2004, 2008). KDE is the most popular approach among researchers and practitioners given its accessibility in mainstream geographic information system software as well as the relatively simple and straightforward interpretation and aesthetic appeal of its outputs. Also, Chainey, Thompson, and Uhlig (2008) and Drawve (2016) found that KDE outperformed other methods by predicting crimes over the smallest geographic areas—though research by Hart and Zandbergen (2012) determined that no single method is superior to another. While spatial exposures to crime are measured by hot spots, spatial vulnerability to crime in a jurisdiction is assessed by RTM to diagnose features of the environment that contribute to the emergence and persistence of crime hot spots.

We have previously explored the "joint utility" of KDE and RTM to predict violence (Caplan, Kennedy, and Piza 2013) and found that both methods produced actionable information that could enhance allocation of police resources. We attributed their high levels of variance explained and other significant findings to the "joint utility" of event-dependent crime prediction techniques that account for prior crime incidence as well as the surrounding environments that facilitate offending and create spatial vulnerabilities. Spatial assessments of exposure incorporated into assessments of vulnerability make better place-based forecasts. This became a key proposition of the theory of risky places, discussed in chapter 5. Hot spot mapping emphasizes a place's history and recent experiences with crime, which serve to aggravate its spatial vulnerability to crime. Building on these findings, we turn our attention to how incorporating KDE and RTM accurately forecasts high-crime micro-places better than either method alone. The purpose of this exercise is to demonstrate the background and significance of our recommended technique for selecting priority target areas for risk-based policing. We conducted the supporting case study, described next, with our research associate Jeremy Barnum.

BROOKLYN AS A CASE STUDY

Brooklyn is a 71-square-mile borough of New York, NY, situated east of Manhattan and south of Queens. It has the largest population of the city's five boroughs, with just over 2.6 million residents, and the second-highest population density, with nearly 37,000 residents per square mile. The focus of this Brooklyn case study is on robbery crimes. Robbery complaints were obtained directly from the New York City Police Department (NYPD) as x-y coordinates and then imported into a geographic information system for preparation and analysis. Here, "robbery" refers only to incidents that occurred in the streets over the course of one year, from October 1, 2014, through September 30, 2015. To make our research operationally meaningful, crime predictions were compared each month and every three months, which are common time intervals for crime analysts to assess ongoing and emerging trends (Santos 2013a).

Consistent with prior research (Chainey, Thompson, and Uhlig 2008; Drawve 2014; Drawve 2016; Dugato 2013), our metric for comparing the individual and combined effects of exposure via KDE and vulnerability via RTM is the prediction accuracy index (PAI). The PAI is a measure of crime prediction accuracy that accounts for the size of the geographic area identified by crime from a previous time period that is required to predict crimes for a subsequent time period (Chainey, Thompson, and Uhlig 2008). It is calculated as:

$$\text{PAI} = \frac{\left(\frac{n}{N}\right) \times 100}{\left(\frac{a}{A}\right) \times 100}$$

where n is the number of robberies in the hot spots or risky places, N is the total number of robberies in the study area, a is the area (in square miles, for example) of the hot spots or risky places, and A is the area of the study area. The numerator is known as the "hit rate," and the denominator as the "area percentage." Higher PAI values indicate better accuracy for a given method, or that more crime is predicted within a smaller geographic area. This metric relates very well to target-area selection for risk-based policing because crime prevention is most efficient when resources are deployed to the smallest number of places that are expected to experience the highest proportion of crimes.

We calculated PAI values at one-month and three-month intervals for KDE, RTM, and a combined measure (based on the two methods) to determine whether accounting for both vulnerability and exposure of places to crime enhances prediction accuracy. More specifically, a PAI value is calculated for each method and for each month (i.e., one month of robbery data to predict the next month's robberies) and for each method every three months (i.e., three months of robbery data to predict the next three months' robberies). This results in a total of 14 time periods (11 one-month intervals and 3 three-month intervals) for which PAI values were calculated and compared for each method.

KDE requires several parameters to be specified *a priori* by the user, including the interpolation method (triangular or quartic), the bandwidth (search radius), and the cell size (Hart and Zandbergen 2014). Both Drawve (2016) and Hart and Zandbergen (2014) found the quartic method to be optimal for crime prediction, which we use here.[1] With regard to bandwidth, Drawve (2016) determined that a 1-block bandwidth produces the highest PAI values. Therefore, we used a 362-foot bandwidth, which approximates the average block length in Brooklyn. Finally, Hart and Zandbergen (2014) found that cell size has little or no effect on PAI values. Therefore, to maintain consistency between the two methods (see discussion below), we used a cell size of 181 feet, which approximates half a block length in Brooklyn.

Each round of KDE utilized robbery incidents in one time period to identify hot spot places that were likely to experience robbery in the subsequent time period. For our purposes, places were considered hot spots if they had kernel density values that were two standard deviations or more above the mean (Caplan, Kennedy, and Piza 2013). Separate KDEs were produced using robbery incidents for each time period to predict robberies in the following time period. For example, for the first time period we used October 2014 robbery incidents to identify hot spots. We then determined the area of October 2014 hot spots relative to the area of Brooklyn and counted the number of November 2014 robbery incidents that fell within them to calculate the PAI values. We continued this process, performing KDE and calculating PAI values for each month through August 2015 (predicting September 2015 incidents). This same process was also completed every three months beginning with October–December 2014 (predicting January–March 2015 incidents) through April–June 2015 (predicting July–September 2015 incidents).

The RTM process began with selecting environmental risk factors for robbery. In total, we included 27 environmental features of the Brooklyn landscape as potential risk factors in each risk terrain model (table 1). Environmental feature data were obtained directly from the NYPD as shapefiles compiled from numerous local government agencies: the Department of Consumer Affairs, Department of Financial Services, Department of City Planning, Department of Environmental Conservation, Department of Information Technology and Telecommunications, Department of Parks and Recreation, New York City Housing Authority, and New York State Liquor Authority.

As was done with KDE, a separate risk terrain model was created each month and every three months to identify places where robbery was likely to happen in the next month and three-month intervals, respectively. For example, for the first month, risk factors were validated and weighted based on October 2014 robbery data to produce risk terrain maps. The resulting high-risk places based on October 2014 risk terrain maps were identified and measured in terms of their area relative to Brooklyn. Finally, the number of November 2014 robbery incidents that fell within the high-risk places was counted to calculate PAI values. We considered places high-risk if their relative risk score, produced by the risk terrain model, was two standard deviations or more above the mean.

TABLE I Environmental Features Included as Potential Risk Factors in Risk Terrain Models of Robbery in Brooklyn

Environmental feature	Observed mean distance (ft.)	Spatial pattern	Operationalization
Banks	517.24	Clustered***	Density and proximity
Billiard halls	5145.17	Random	Proximity
Check cashing businesses	2071.86	Dispersed***	Proximity
Chemical dependency facilities	1207.40	Clustered***	Density and proximity
Cinemas	4140.73	Random	Proximity
Clubs	2924.96	Random	Proximity
Colleges and universities	3445.80	Random	Proximity
Food pantries and soup kitchens	1252.81	Clustered***	Density and proximity
Gas stations	1025.96	Clustered***	Density and proximity
Grocery stores	307.17	Clustered***	Density and proximity
Homeless facilities	1486.28	Clustered***	Density and proximity
Hospitals	4708.05	Random	Proximity
Hotels and motels	1772.22	Clustered***	Density and proximity
Laundromats	353.58	Clustered***	Density and proximity
Mental health facilities	787.05	Clustered***	Density and proximity
Developments†	–	–	Proximity
Off premise liquor establishments	757.69	Clustered***	Density and proximity
On premise liquor establishments	293.92	Clustered***	Density and proximity
Parking facilities	799.24	Clustered***	Density and proximity
Parks†	–	–	Proximity
Pawnbrokers and secondhand dealers	264.08	Clustered***	Density and proximity
Pharmacies	604.54	Clustered***	Density and proximity
Postal facilities	2795.17	Dispersed*	Proximity
Schools	551.47	Clustered***	Density and proximity
Recreation centers	9712.50	Dispersed***	Proximity
Restaurants	477.43	Clustered***	Density and proximity
Subway entrances	176.49	Clustered***	Density and proximity

*$p < 0.05$; ***$p < 0.001$.

† This risk factor was converted from a polygon to points for use in RTMDx. Thus, the operationalization was set to proximity only.

This statistically approximates the top 5% of highest-risk places. We also completed this process every three months beginning with October–December 2014 (predicting January–March 2015 incidents) through April–June 2015 (predicting July–September 2015 incidents).

All risk terrain models were created in the RTMDx software (Caplan and Kennedy 2013). As with KDE, we specified a cell size of 181 feet and a block length of 362 feet (the average block length in Brooklyn) as parameters for the RTM analysis (Caplan, Kennedy, and Piza, 2013). Additional parameters for the RTM included operationalization, maximum spatial influence, and analysis increments. We tested the spatial influence of each environmental feature to a maximum extent of 3 blocks. Analysis increments refer to the level of detail at which spatial influence is assessed (i.e., half-block or whole-block increments). We tested the spatial influence of each environmental feature at half-block increments to more precisely specify the dynamics of spatial influence across the landscape.

For each KDE or RTM analysis, Brooklyn was represented as a grid of 181-foot by 181-foot cells ($n = 61,361$). Each cell represented a micro-place that may have been identified, during each one month or three month period, as a hot spot via KDE or a high-risk place via RTM. To evaluate the co-effects of the two methods, we used a simple Boolean approach to create an integrated measure of exposure and vulnerability.[2] For cells that were both hot spots and high-risk places, we measured their area relative to Brooklyn and counted the number of robberies in the subsequent time period to calculate PAI values. The PAI values were then compared across all three approaches to determine whether robbery predictions improved when jointly considering the outputs of both approaches relative to those of the individual methods. The results are presented graphically in figures 6 and 7.

Considering the methods individually, the PAI values suggest that RTM tends to outperform KDE in terms of prediction accuracy. In 7 of the 11 months, RTM produced a higher PAI value. The average PAI value for RTM across all months was also higher than the average KDE value. The results of three-month intervals tell a similar story. In all three time periods, RTM produced a higher PAI value, and the average PAI value for RTM across all three time periods was significantly higher than the KDE average. This is similar to findings reported by Drawve (2016).

The findings here reinforce the notion that spatial crime predictions are most accurate when considering both aspects—crime vulnerability and exposure—at places. Whereas KDE provides a measure of exposure to crime, RTM identifies a location's vulnerability to illegal behavior. The vulnerability–exposure framework enhances spatial crime prediction at micro-places, and thereby supports selecting target areas for risk-based policing that give priority to high-risk places that intersect with recent crime hot spots. As resources permit, risk-based policing efforts can expand from these priority areas to all other high-risk places throughout the jurisdiction.

RTM and KDE clearly have unique and meaningful utility for crime analysis. But the PAI values were greatest when considering vulnerable *and* exposed locations at once.

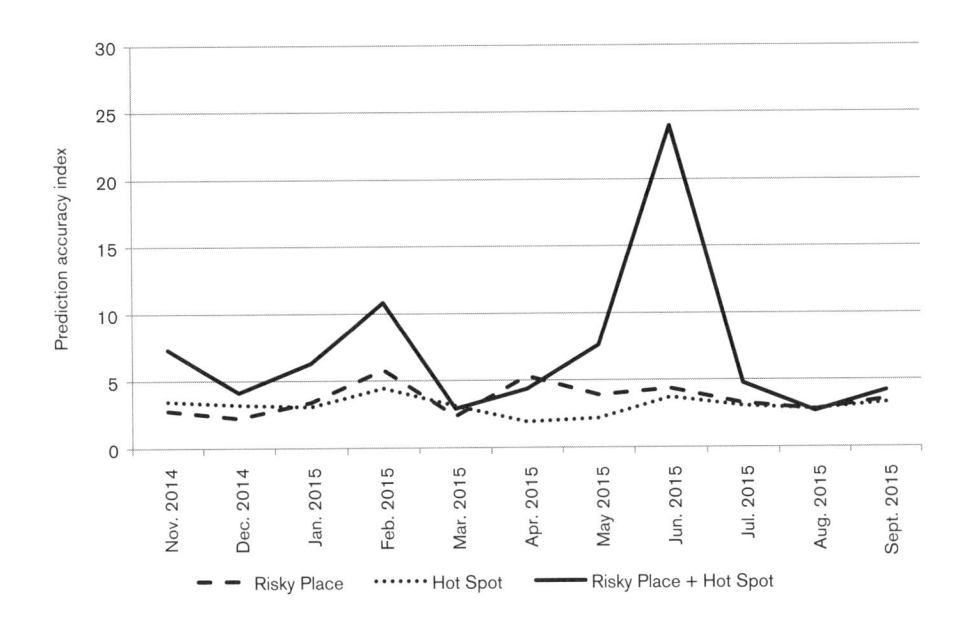

FIGURE 6
Monthly prediction accuracy index for risk terrain modeling, kernel density estimation, and the integrated approach.

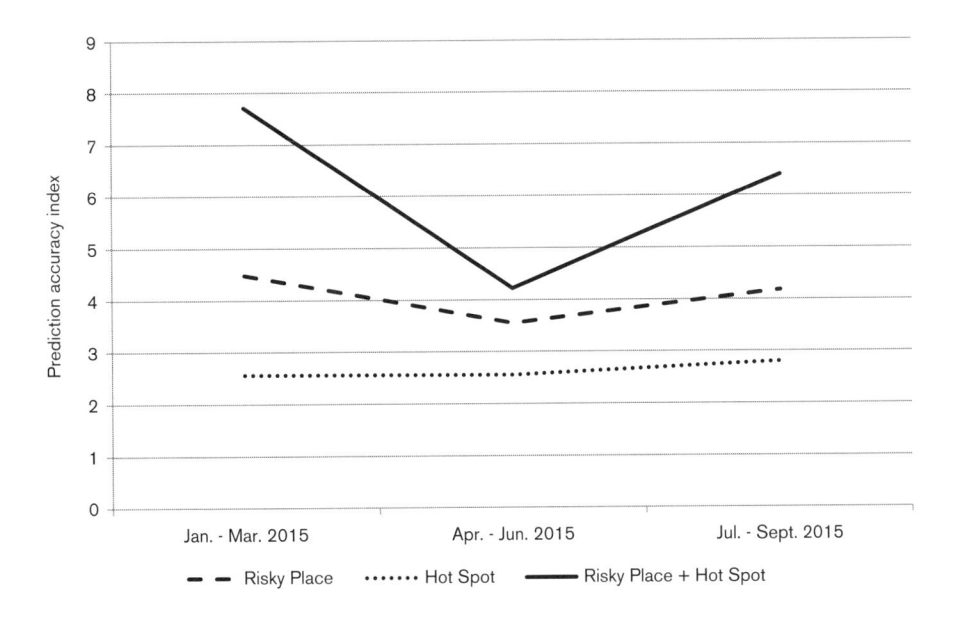

FIGURE 7
Quarterly prediction accuracy index for risk terrain modeling, kernel density estimation, and the integrated approach.

Overall, the joint approach produced PAI values that were twice as high as KDE or RTM alone. These results are consistent with the theory of risky places as originally proposed by Kennedy et al. (2016), but advance their research findings by demonstrating the implicit value of integrating these methods into a unified measure for target area definition. KDE identifies places where crime has concentrated in the past but does not account for the collection of environmental features that may have facilitated offending or sustained its persistence. RTM measures vulnerability by accounting for the presence of environmental features that create conditions suitable to offending, but it is limited by the potential that high-risk places may never be known to motivated offenders or used for criminal activities in the face of other places that are currently well-known or "reputable" options. Integrating the two techniques yields actionable information that can be used to anticipate new crime places with great efficiency (Garnier et al. 2018).

CONCLUSION

Risk-based policing activities aimed at crime prevention and risk reduction should focus on high-risk places, identified by RTM, and prioritize these target areas that intersect crime hot spots. This evidence-based insight is offered here as a practical way for police leaders to select and prioritize target areas for risk-based policing. The efficiency of police operations can be increased by maximizing risk reduction efforts at the particular places most likely to experience crime problems, while minimizing the number and geographic area of target locations. This chapter demonstrated that a higher proportion of crime could be predicted in the most minimal geographic areas when considering both spatial vulnerabilities and exposures to crime. This enhances the strategic and tactical allocation of resources and risk reduction actions intended to deter illegal behavior and prevent crime.

NOTES

1. We used ArcGIS to perform each KDE, which by default employs interpolation based on the quartic method.

2. In ArcGIS, we created a single grid of cells with the same size and dimension as the grids employed in the KDE and RTM analyses. In the accompanying attributes table, we created separate columns to indicate whether each cell was considered a hot spot or high-risk place during each time period. Then for each time period, we "selected by attributes" cells that were considered both hot spots *and* high-risk places.

7

THE ROLE OF POLICE IN RISK-BASED POLICING
Case Studies of Colorado Springs, Glendale, Newark, and Kansas City

> **KEY POINTS**
> - Police using risk-based approaches tailor the information they get from assessments to become problem-solvers and to develop successful interventions.
> - Interventions need to be continually assessed for impacts on police practice and desired outcomes.
> - Case studies document successes and provide evidence for new intervention strategies.

INTRODUCTION

Police like to problem-solve, but they need the right information. Implementing risk reduction strategies at high-risk places takes the assessment stage of risk-based policing to the next level. This happens through identifying high-risk places and deploying preventative patrols. It also involves planning and carrying out multifaceted strategies to mitigate environmental attractors of crime located there. In this chapter, we use examples of research completed in four cities: Colorado Springs, CO, Glendale, AZ, Kansas City, MO, and Newark, NJ. With support from the National Institute of Justice of the U.S. Department of Justice, we conducted a scientific experiment that had two primary goals: to validate risk terrain modeling (RTM) in multiple jurisdictions and across many different crime types; and to evaluate risk reduction intervention strategies targeted at high-risk places across several cities. The practical steps of evaluating the impact of these police-led interventions are reviewed and explained in detail. Adopting risk-based policing in a police agency does not require this level of rigorous research. We present it here, however, to demonstrate the evidence-based nature of risk-based policing and to convey the crime reduction success that is possible in any jurisdiction that employs it. We begin this chapter with a detailed review of RTM analysis and the success of each intervention in the four jurisdictions. In chapter 8, we provide an overview of the step-by-step implementation process using a planned change model (Welsh and Harris 2016).

RISK ASSESSMENT METHODOLOGY

RTMDx software was used to produce risk terrain models for each jurisdiction studied. The software, produced at Rutgers University by the Rutgers Center on Public Security, applies a precise set of statistical tests in evaluating the relative importance of spatial factors in influencing crime outcomes (Caplan, Kennedy, and Piza 2013). It begins by building an elastic net penalized regression model, assuming a Poisson distribution of events. It does this using cross-validation. Then it further simplifies the model in subsequent steps via a bidirectional stepwise regression process (Poisson and negative binomial) and measures the Bayesian information criterion (BIC) score. The model with the lowest BIC score between Poisson and negative binomial distributions is selected. RTMDx outputs are tabular and cartographic; for each significant risk factor, tabular outputs include a relative risk value, which is the exponentiated factor coefficient (i.e., relative weight), and the optimal operationalization and distal extent of spatial influence. A risk terrain map is also produced to show high-risk places throughout the study area.

Following the RTM analyses for each city in this research project, police officers from each department developed an intervention strategy that aimed to mitigate the spatial influences of selected risk factors. The police departments also worked with the research team in the selection of target areas for the intervention activities. In evaluating the intervention, statistical comparisons were made to equivalent control areas locally within each city. Control areas were matched to treatment areas through propensity score matching (PSM). PSM helps approximate the conditions of a randomized controlled trial by ensuring statistical equivalency of treatment and control groups. In each evaluation, the units of analysis were street segments and street intersections, which we refer to as "street units." For each city, the PSM technique balanced treatment and control units on the following variables:

- whether the street unit *intersected a high-risk cell* as identified by the RTM analysis;
- whether the street unit *intersected a high-risk street unit* for the purpose of identifying risk clusters;
- the *concentrated social disadvantage* of the surrounding 2010 U.S. Census block group;

TABLE 2 Colorado Springs Propensity Score Matching

Variable	Treatment	Control	S.E.	T-stat	% bias	% bias red.
High-risk unit						
Unmatched	0.4	0.2	0.0	5.2**	42.2	
Matched	0.4	0.4	0.1	1.0	12.2	71.0
Intersects high-risk unit						
Unmatched	0.7	0.4	0.0	7.7**	68.8	
Matched	0.7	0.6	0.1	0.9	10.3	85.1
Social deprivation						
Unmatched	1.9	0.0	0.3	7.1**	69.2	
Matched	1.9	2.1	0.3	−0.7	−8.9	87.1
Racial heterogeneity						
Unmatched	0.1	0.1	0.0	1.0	9.6	
Matched	0.1	0.1	0.0	−0.5	−6.1	36.2
Pre-intervention crime count						
Unmatched	0.4	0.4	0.1	−0.7	−5.9	
Matched	0.4	0.4	0.1	−0.4	−4.5	24.1
Proactive police actions						
Unmatched	6.7	7.2	4.2	−0.1	−1.6	
Matched	6.7	7.6	1.8	−0.5	−2.5	−55.1
Street segment						
Unmatched	0.9	1.0	0.0	−2.1*	−15.6	
Matched	1.0	0.9	0.0	0.5	7.1	54.4

NOTE: PSM algorithm: nearest neighbor, caliper = 0.01.
**$p < 0.01$, *$p < 0.05$.

- the *racial heterogeneity* of the surrounding 2010 U.S. Census block group;
- the *pre-intervention period crime count*;
- the *pre-intervention period count of proactive police actions*; and
- whether the street unit was a *street segment* or *street intersection*.

Covariate balance was assessed through independent sample *t*-tests (Dehejia and Wahba 1999) and estimation of the standardized bias (Rosenbaum and Rubin 1985). As a rule of thumb, when the *t*-test $p > 0.05$ and bias < 20 percent, statistical equivalency is achieved (Austin, Grootendorst, and Anderson 2007), which we observed for each city. The findings of the PSM algorithms for each city are presented in tables 2–5 with the balance achieved for each city.

TABLE 3 Glendale Propensity Score Matching

Variable	Treatment	Control	S.E.	T-stat	% bias	% bias red.
High-risk unit						
Unmatched	0.76	0.45	0.09	3.61**	66.00	92.90
Matched	0.73	0.71	0.09	0.24	4.70	
Intersects high-risk unit						
Unmatched	0.10	0.15	0.06	–0.89	–16.30	75.80
Matched	0.11	0.10	0.07	0.20	4.00	
Social deprivation						
Unmatched	1.96	0.44	0.55	2.78**	50.50	97.20
Matched	1.71	1.76	0.58	–0.07	–1.40	
Racial heterogeneity						
Unmatched	0.79	0.56	0.19	1.19	19.40	78.60
Matched	0.70	0.75	0.24	–0.20	–4.10	
Pre-intervention crime count						
Unmatched	3.14	1.13	0.53	3.80**	54.60	94.50
Matched	1.76	1.87	0.47	–0.23	–3.00	
Proactive police actions						
Unmatched	0.76	0.45	0.09	3.61**	66.00	92.90
Matched	0.73	0.71	0.09	0.24	4.70	

NOTE: PSM algorithm: Epanechnikov kernel.
**$p < 0.01$, *$p < 0.05$.

Post-matching, we tested both counts and crime change scores as the dependent variables, with the two models showing similar results. Here, we present crime change scores because they are more meaningful for our operational definition of "effect" on crime. Two separate analyses were executed for each city: a target-area-wide analysis tested the aggregate intervention effect, and a micro-level analysis tested the effect of the intervention and disaggregated intervention activities at the street-unit level. The target-area-wide effect was reported as a relative effect size (RES).[1] Variance of the RES was calculated from the variance of the natural logarithm of RES.[2] And for each significant RES suggestive of a crime reduction, we calculated a weighted displacement quotient to test for spatial displacement.[3]

The micro-level analysis measured intervention effect on the street-unit level, as opposed to the entire target area. First, we measured the average treatment effect on the treated (ATT), which is defined as "the expected effect of treatment for those individuals actually assigned to the treatment group, or the 'gain' from treatment among those in the treated group" (Apel and Sweeten 2010, 545). While crime-level changes across the entire

TABLE 4 Newark Propensity Score Matching

Variable	Treatment	Control	S.E.	T-stat	% bias	% bias red.
High-risk unit						
Unmatched	0.24	0.10	0.03	5.46**	39.00	66.40
Matched	0.23	0.18	0.05	0.99	13.10	
Intersects high-risk unit						
Unmatched	0.57	0.25	0.04	8.83**	68.70	83.20
Matched	0.56	0.61	0.05	−0.89	−11.50	
Social deprivation						
Unmatched	−1.92	1.30	0.31	−10.27**	−95.70	93.00
Matched	−1.90	−1.67	0.34	−0.67	−6.70	
Racial heterogeneity						
Unmatched	0.09	0.08	0.00	2.90**	23.70	80.80
Matched	0.09	0.10	0.00	−0.39	−4.60	
Pre-intervention crime count						
Unmatched	0.36	0.42	0.05	−1.40	−11.40	40.60
Matched	0.35	0.39	0.07	−0.57	−6.70	
Proactive police actions						
Unmatched	3.72	3.08	0.61	1.05	8.80	−115.40
Matched	3.58	4.94	−1.36	−1.49	−18.80	
Street segment						
Unmatched	0.55	0.71	0.04	−4.35**	−34.40	58.80
Matched	0.56	0.49	0.06	1.12	14.20	

NOTE: Propensity score algorithm: 2 nearest neighbors matching, caliper = .01.
**$p < 0.01$, *$p < 0.05$.

target area reflect the cumulative effect of the intervention, the ATT measures whether intervention effect was experienced across all of the micro-places (e.g. street units) that comprise the target area.

Following the ATT analysis, a regression analysis further tested the influence of the intervention actions on crime-level changes at street units. In each model, crime count change from pre- to during/post-intervention period was the dependent variable, and each disaggregate intervention action was an independent variable. Control variables included a dichotomous variable denoting whether each observation was in the treatment group (1) or the control group (0); the pre-period crime count; a dichotomous variable denoting whether each observation was a street segment (1) or a street intersection (0); and the observation's propensity score. When the dependent variable was normally

TABLE 5 Kansas City Propensity Score Matching

Variable	Treatment	Control	S.E.	T-stat	% bias	% bias red.
High-risk unit						
Unmatched	0.53	0.40	0.04	2.89**	24.70	32.30
Matched	0.53	0.44	0.06	1.35	16.70	
Intersects high-risk unit						
Unmatched	0.83	0.54	0.04	6.70**	64.60	92.50
Matched	0.83	0.85	0.05	−0.45	−4.90	
Social deprivation						
Unmatched	−0.40	1.05	0.34	−4.21**	41.70	79.80
Matched	−0.40	−0.10	0.36	−0.82	−8.40	
Racial heterogeneity						
Unmatched	0.08	0.08	0.00	0.90	8.00	85.10
Matched	0.08	0.08	0.00	0.00	−1.20	
Pre-intervention crime count						
Unmatched	0.25	0.48	0.07	−3.21**	−33.90	64.50
Matched	0.25	0.33	0.06	−1.32	−12.10	
Proactive police actions						
Unmatched	2.29	1.88	0.42	0.99	8.60	−116.10
Matched	2.29	3.19	0.74	−1.21	−18.60	
Street segment						
Unmatched	0.63	0.63	0.04	0.06	0.60	−1,658.80
Matched	0.63	0.59	0.06	0.78	9.70	

NOTE: Propensity score algorithm: 2 nearest neighbors matching, caliper = .01.
**$p < 0.01$, *$p < 0.05$.

distributed, ordinary least square regression models were used. For skewed distributions, ordinal logistic regression models were used, with the dependent variable treated as an ordinal measure rather than continuous. In the next section, we present a summary of the findings for each city.[4]

FINDINGS

COLORADO SPRINGS

Colorado Springs is the second-largest city in Colorado (behind Denver), with an estimated 2014 population of 445,830. It is a largely middle-class city, with a median household income of $53,962 and poverty level of 13.7 percent, reflective of the economic

TABLE 6 Colorado Springs Significant Risk Factors

Risk factor	Operationalization	Spatial influence	Coefficient	Relative risk value
Disorder calls-for-service	Density	1 block	1.72	5.61
Multifamily housing units	Proximity	3 blocks	1.01	2.75
Foreclosures	Proximity	3 blocks	0.97	2.64
Parks	Proximity	3 blocks	0.56	1.76
Sit-down restaurants	Proximity	3 blocks	0.41	1.51
Commercial zoning	Proximity	3 blocks	0.31	1.37

condition of Colorado as a whole (median income of $58,433 and poverty rate of 13.2 percent). Approximately 79 percent of residents are White, with Blacks accounting for 6.3 percent of the population. Hispanic or Latino residents constituted 16.1 percent (U.S. Census Bureau 2015).

The Colorado Springs Police Department (CSPD) selected motor vehicle theft (MVT) as its priority crime for the risk-based intervention. Colorado Springs reported 2,673 MVT incidents during the study period, a rate of 599.55 per 100,000 residents. This rate is above the national average of 420.90 per 100,000 for U.S. cities with populations greater than 250,000, per Uniform Crime Report figures (Federal Bureau of Investigation 2014). In Colorado, the MVT rate for Colorado Springs is the second-highest in the state, behind only Denver (Federal Bureau of Investigation 2014). The CSPD has been recognized as one of the national leaders of problem-oriented policing in the US (Maguire, Uchida, and Hassell 2015), with a long history of commitment to research and evaluation.

The spatial influences of 19 potential risk factors were tested with RTM: malls; parking stations and garages; retail shops; bowling centers; convenience stores; foreclosures; gas stations with convenience stores; hotels and motels; liquor stores; night clubs; sit-down restaurants; take-out restaurants; variety stores; bars; disorder calls-for-service (citizen initiated); multifamily housing units; parks; schools; and commercial zoning. All geographic calculations were conducted using raster cells (i.e., units of analysis) of 276 feet and an average block length of 552 feet. There were 77,873 raster cells used in the analysis, of which 1,465 cells contained events. A significant risk terrain model for MVT was found that contained six risk factors: disorder calls-for-service (RRV = 5.61), multifamily housing units (RRV = 2.75), foreclosures (RRV = 2.64), parks (RRV = 1.76), sit-down restaurants (RRV = 1.51), and commercial zoning (RRV = 1.37) (table 6). Figure 8 displays a map of the final RTM in Colorado Springs.

CSPD's risk-based intervention began May 1, 2014, and ended August 15, 2014. To reflect the RTM findings, CSPD designed its intervention strategies to address incidents of disorder. An array of activities were performed by various CSPD units to prioritize disorder problems in the target area. The activities included code enforcement property

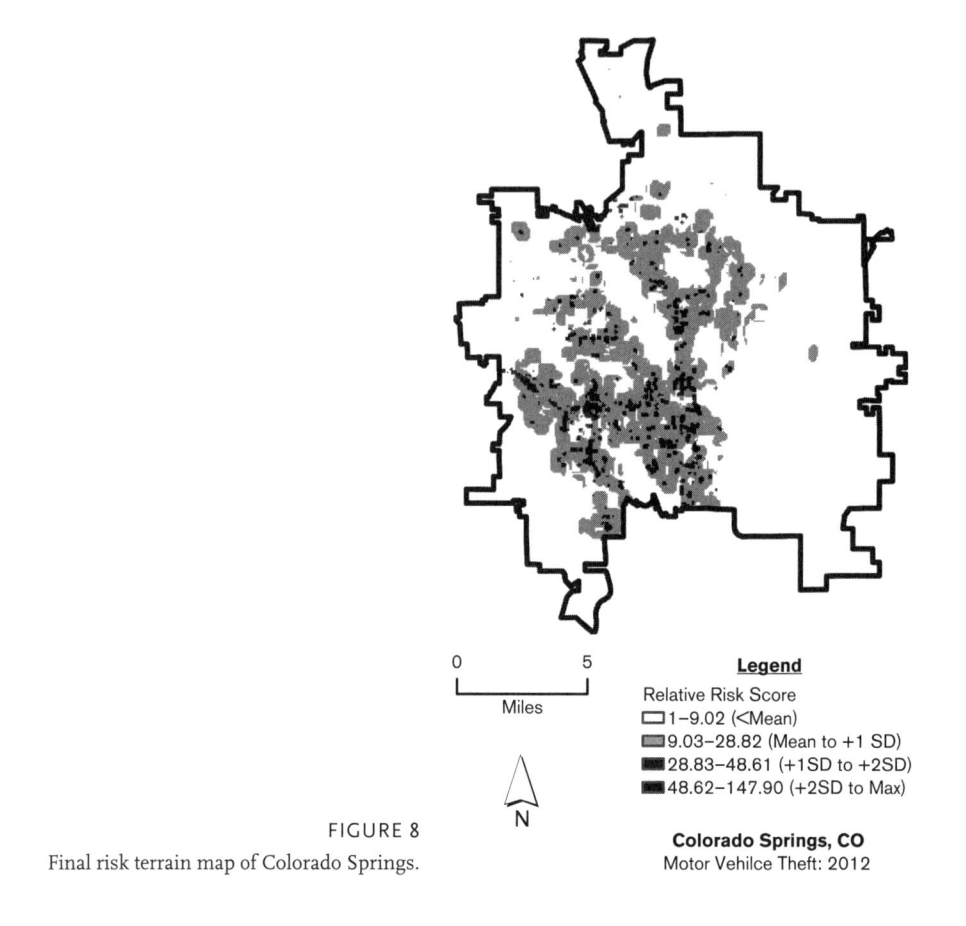

FIGURE 8
Final risk terrain map of Colorado Springs.

Legend
Relative Risk Score
☐ 1–9.02 (<Mean)
▨ 9.03–28.82 (Mean to +1 SD)
▨ 28.83–48.61 (+1SD to +2SD)
▨ 48.62–147.90 (+2SD to Max)

Colorado Springs, CO
Motor Vehilce Theft: 2012

inspections, community service officer neighborhood cleanups, community meetings, proactive enforcement against disorder offenses, proactive traffic enforcement, and the deployment of license plate recognition (LPR) devices to identify stolen motor vehicles in the target area (figure 9).

CSPD was able to provide incident-specific data for each intervention activity except the LPR deployment. We were told that LPR units were deployed each day of the intervention period within the Sand Creek Division, the intervention target area. However, no additional information was provided on the locations, times, or number of stolen motor vehicles detected by LPR. This presented a challenge for the evaluation. The deployment of LPR increased the likelihood that stolen vehicles would be identified and reported in the target area. Therefore, we decided not to measure intervention effect during the intervention, instead focusing on the time period immediately following the intervention. This follows the approach of prior evaluations of police interventions that may have generated more opportunities for crime to be reported by citizens and/or discovered by police (e.g. Braga et al. 1999; Weisburd and Green 1995). For the current

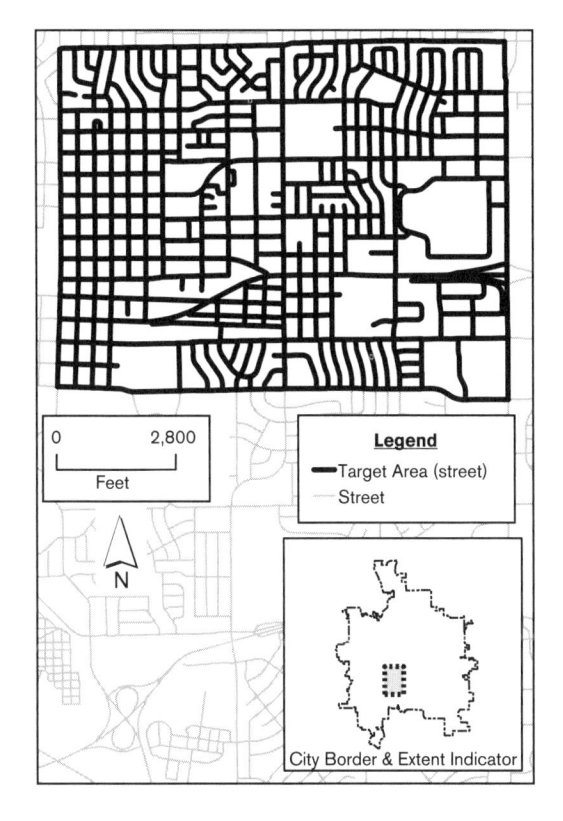

FIGURE 9
Colorado Springs Police Department risk-based intervention target area.

study, the post-intervention period of August 16 through November 30, 2014, was compared to the same time period in the previous year to control for seasonality.

The analysis began with a fidelity check to ensure that intervention activities were confined to the target area. This is an important consideration since prior research has found that police officers may not adhere to target-area boundaries, which could threaten the validity of empirical evaluations (Sorg et al. 2014). As displayed in table 7, approximately 97 percent (836 of 864) of intervention activities occurred in the target area. The approximately 3 percent of activities outside the target area occurred across 18 street units in the catchment zones. These 18 catchment zone street units were excluded from the analysis to prevent contamination of results.

Table 8 displays results of the macro-level (i.e., target-area-wide) analysis. Crime counts were reported for both the treatment and control areas. Treatment units were matched with control units via a nearest neighbor PSM model with a caliper of 0.01. Results show a MVT reduction of 33 percent in the target area as compared to the control area during the three-month post-intervention period. There was also a diffusion of benefits to nearby areas. According to the ATT findings in table 9, target-area street units experienced a crime count reduction that, on average, was greater than that experienced

TABLE 7   CSPD Intervention Activities, Fidelity Check

Type	In target area	Not in target area	Total
Code enforcement	48	0	48
CSO cleanup	370	5	375
Community meetings	3	0	3
Proactive enforcement	127	12	139
Traffic enforcement	288	11	299
Total	*836*	*28*	*864*

NOTE: All actions not in target area occurred across 18 street units in the catchment zone.

TABLE 8   CSPD Macro-Level Crime Change, Post-intervention

Group	Post	Pre – Post	RES	Var(RES)	SE	WDQ	Phi
Treatment	51	75	1.50^	0.08	0.29	0.45	0.06
Control	58	57					
Catchment	64	74					
N *treatment*	144						
N control	144						

NOTE: PSM algorithm: nearest neighbor, caliper = 0.01.
^$p < 0.10$

TABLE 9   CSPD Average Treatment Effect on the Treated (ATT)

Crime	ATT	SE
Motor vehicle theft (post-intervention)	−0.17*	0.10

NOTE: Bootstrapped standard errors with 50 replications are provided.
*$p < 0.05$

in the matched control unit. So, while the entirety of the target area experienced a statistically significant crime reduction, some places in the target area may have received greater impacts than others. The purpose of the micro-level analysis presented in table 10 was to measure the effect of the disaggregate intervention activities on the occurrence of MVT. As per model 1, code enforcement was associated with reduced levels of MVT throughout the target area. In fact, model 2 reveals that code enforcement activities have an exceptionally strong and significant crime reduction benefit at high-risk places.

TABLE 10 CSPD Regression Models, Post-intervention Period

Dependent variable = crime change score

Covariate	Model 1: Overall activities			Model 2: High-risk activities		
	Coeff.	S.E.	p	Coeff.	S.E.	p
Treatment	−0.05	0.07	0.50	−0.08	0.07	0.28
Code enforcement	−0.38	0.07	0.00	−0.44	0.15	0.00
CSO-community meetings	0.01	0.01	0.10	0.03	0.06	0.65
Proactive enforcement	0.03	0.05	0.53	0.18	0.12	0.14
Traffic enforcement	−0.01	0.01	0.49	0.00	0.04	0.93
Pre-crime count	−1.05	0.07	0.00	−1.03	0.06	0.00
Segment	−0.12	0.16	0.48	−0.13	0.16	0.44
Pscore	0.16	0.34	0.65	0.13	0.34	0.70
Constant	0.50	0.19	0.01	0.50	0.19	0.01
r^2	0.61			0.60		

The cumulative findings suggest that CSPD's risk-based intervention effectively addressed MVT. The macro-level analysis found a statistically significant reduction of MVT throughout the target area. This suggests that CSPD's targeting of disorder incidents was an effective crime control strategy, which concurs with recent research findings that disorder-related policing can generate significant crime reductions (Braga, Welsh, and Schnell 2015; Kondo et al. 2015). The micro-level analysis suggests that code enforcement focused at micro-level high-risk places is a particularly promising tactic. Given the negative connotations often associated with policing disorder offenses, it is worth noting that CSPD instituted an innovative application of policing these types of offenses and related calls-for-service located in the high-risk areas that included more than merely "law enforcement" actions. In this regard, a summons was issued in only 10 of the 139 instances of police dealings with these types of offenders. No arrests occurred. The majority of incidents were handled via non-punitive actions (verbal warnings, etc.).

GLENDALE

Glendale, in Maricopa County, Arizona, has a residential population of 226,721, according to the decennial census. Glendale hosts a number of visitors from outside the city due to the presence of the University of Phoenix stadium. In addition to being a venue for regular concerts and other entertainment events, the stadium is home to the National Football League's Arizona Cardinals and has hosted the Super Bowl twice, in 2008 and 2015. Glendale is a majority-White city (67.8 percent) with a Black population of 6 percent; 35.5 percent of residents identify as Hispanic or Latino. Glendale has a median household income of $46,776, compared to $50,255 for the state of Arizona.

FIGURE 10
Final risk terrain map of Glendale.

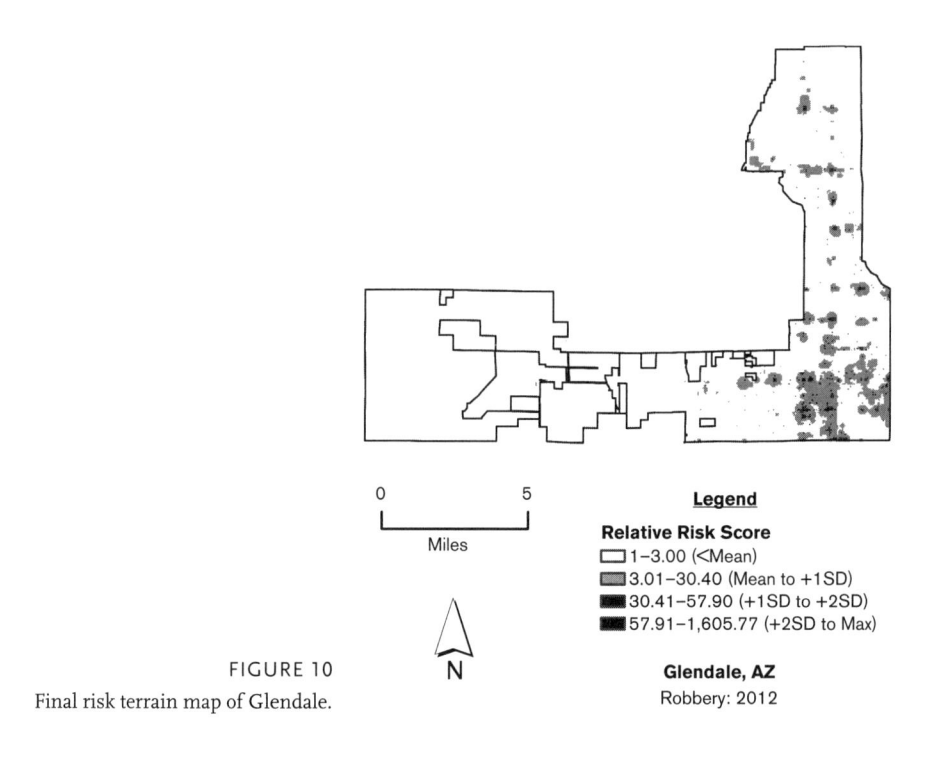

Glendale, AZ
Robbery: 2012

Legend
Relative Risk Score
☐ 1–3.00 (<Mean)
▨ 3.01–30.40 (Mean to +1SD)
■ 30.41–57.90 (+1SD to +2SD)
■ 57.91–1,605.77 (+2SD to Max)

Glendale had experienced a progressive decrease in violent crimes over the last few years prior to this research study. From 2011 to 2012 the rate of murders diminished by 45 percent. However, Glendale's persistent high rates of property crimes have remained a major issue. The rate of larceny-theft events increased during those years by more than 9 percent. In absolute terms the rate of property crimes can be considered very high, with 64.5 incidents per 1,000 residents. In the context of high property-crime rates, the Glendale PD had some experience with interventions and had put into place (prior to the risk-based initiative) a series of programs that it claimed reduced thefts in Glendale. The Smart Policing Initiative serves as an illustration of this effort. It was a problem-oriented policing program that targeted Circle K stores, a chain of convenience stores with disproportionately high numbers of police calls-for-service. The program used geographic information system analysis to map call activity at convenience stores. The results from this study shed some light on the reasons why theft-related incidents were higher in this particular chain compared to others.

The Glendale Police Department (GPD) identified robbery as its priority crime for the risk-based policing initiative. The analysis began with a risk terrain model of robbery in 2012. The spatial influences of eleven risk factors were tested with RTMDx: bars, liquor stores, restaurants with liquor licenses, drug-related calls-for-service, apartment complexes, parks, gang-member residences, convenience stores, take-out restaurants, ATMs, and gas stations. All geographic calculations were conducted using raster cells (i.e., units

TABLE 11 Glendale Significant Risk Factors

Risk factor	Operationalization	Spatial influence	Coefficient	Relative risk value
Drug-related calls-for-service	Density	Half-block	2.74	15.56
Convenience stores	Proximity	1 block	1.06	2.88
Take-out restaurants	Proximity	1 block	0.93	2.54
Apartment complexes	Proximity	3 blocks	0.93	2.53
Gang-member residences	Density	2 blocks	0.88	2.41
Liquor stores	Density	3 blocks	0.83	2.30
Bars	Proximity	1 block	0.78	2.19

of analysis) of 236 feet and an average block length of 472 feet. There were 31,197 raster cells used in the analysis, of which 277 cells contained events.

A risk terrain model for robbery was found that contains seven risk factors: drug-related calls-for-service (RRV = 15.56), convenience stores (RRV = 2.88), take-out restaurants (RRV = 2.54), apartment complexes (RRV = 2.53), gang-member residences (RRV = 2.41), liquor stores (RRV = 2.30), and bars (RRV = 2.19) (table 11). Figure 10 displays a map of the final RTM in Glendale.

GPD's risk-based intervention began September 15, 2013, and ended December 15, 2013. To reflect the RTM findings, GPD designed its intervention strategy to address all seven risk factors. An array of activities were conducted by GPD to mitigate the spatial influences of these risk factors, enhance community awareness, and deter motivated offenders. The activities included directed patrols, flyer distribution, community meetings, public engagement activities, proactive meet-and-greets, and law enforcement actions. We were interested in two different time frames for the evaluation: the 90-day intervention period (during which intervention activities were carried out) and the 90-day post-intervention period. Each period was compared to the same time period from the previous year to control for seasonality.

Table 12 presents a fidelity check measuring whether the intervention activities were confined to the target area (see figure 11). A higher proportion of intervention activities occurred outside the target area in Glendale than in any other of the project cities. In total, approximately 9 percent (175 of 1850) of activities occurred outside the target area. Furthermore, these 175 actions occurred across 59 prospective control street segments. Since the within-target-area actions were confined to only 81 street segments, the number of outside-target-area street segments subjected to intervention actions shows that the target-area boundaries were not strictly adhered to. Therefore, we considered each street segment that experienced at least one intervention action as the "target areas" for the evaluation, as this was considered a better measure of program implementation than the predetermined target area.

FIGURE 11
Glendale Police Department risk-based intervention target area.

TABLE 12 GPD Intervention Activities Fidelity Check

Type	In target area	Not in target area	Total
Arrests	21	8	29
Flyer distribution	658	44	702
Community engagement	502	47	549
Proactive stops	65	18	83
Directed patrols	415	50	465
Other	14	8	22
Total	*1675*	*175*	*1850*

NOTE: 175 intervention actions occurred across 59 prospective control street segments.

TABLE 13 GPD Macro-Level Crime Changes during Intervention

Group	During	Pre	RES	Var(RES)	S.E.	WDQ	Phi
Treatment	12	26	1.73^	0.18	0.43	3.45	0.08
Control	63	79					
N Treatment	37						
N Control	141						

TABLE 14 GPD Macro-Level Crime Changes Post-intervention

Group	Post	Pre – post	RES	Var(RES)	SE
Treatment	29	21	0.72	0.16	0.40
Control	43	52			
N treatment	37				
N control	141				

TABLE 15 GPD Average Treatment Effect on the Treated (ATT)

Crime	ATT	SE
Robbery (during intervention)	0.00	0.26
Robbery (post-intervention)	0.35	0.34

NOTE: Bootstrapped standard errors with 50 replications are provided.

Table 13 displays the results of the macro-level (i.e., target-area-wide) analysis for the during-intervention period. Table 14 displays the ATT findings. Crime counts were reported for both the treatment and control areas. Treatment units were matched with control units via an Epanechnikov kernel PSM model. The results show that robbery decreased by 42 percent in the target area as compared to the control area. There was also a diffusion of benefits to nearby places. Results of the macro-level (i.e., target-area-wide) analysis for the post-intervention period, presented in table 15, suggest that the risk reduction activities had the most impact while they were sustained, compared to after they were stopped at the conclusion of the test period. The purpose of the micro-level analyses presented in table 16 (during-intervention period) and table 17 (post-intervention period) was to measure the effect of the disaggregate intervention activities on the occurrence of robbery. In the during-intervention analysis, directed patrols were associated with lower levels of robbery. In the post-intervention analysis, flyer distribution activities were associated with lower levels of robbery.

TABLE 16   GPD Regression Models during Intervention Period

Dependent variable = crime change score

	Model 1: Overall activities			Model 2: High-risk activities		
Covariate	*Coeff.*	*S.E.*	p	*Coeff.*	*S.E.*	p
Treatment	−0.45	0.55	0.41	−0.31	0.47	0.51
Arrests	−0.05	0.73	0.95	−0.32	0.59	0.58
Flyer distribution	0.01	0.05	0.17	−0.3	0.03	0.42
Community engagement	−0.01	0.04	0.89	−0.01	0.02	0.48
Proactive stops	−0.08	0.14	0.57	−0.04	0.62	0.50
Directed patrols	−0.09	0.05	0.09	0.04	0.04	0.36
Pre-crime count	−5.04	0.91	0.00	−5.04	0.92	0.00
Pscore	−0.02	1.19	0.99	0.16	1.19	0.89
r^2	0.45			0.45		

TABLE 17   GPD Regression Models, Post-intervention Period

Dependent variable = crime change score

	Model 1: Overall activities			Model 2: High-risk activities		
Covariate	*Coeff.*	*S.E.*	p	*Coeff.*	*S.E.*	p
Treatment	0.07	0.16	0.65	0.13	0.14	0.35
Arrests	0.66	0.44	0.13	0.33	0.28	0.24
Flyer distribution	−0.04	0.03	0.09	−0.02	0.02	0.29
Community engagement	0.06	0.04	0.11	0.03	0.02	0.12
Proactive stops	0.00	0.09	0.98	0.01	0.05	0.85
Directed patrols	0.03	0.02	0.27	0.01	0.03	0.60
Pre-crime count	−1.21	0.08	0.00	−1.17	0.07	0.00
Pscore	0.76	0.45	0.09	0.69	0.46	0.14
Constant	0.23	0.10	0.02	0.23	0.10	0.02
r^2	0.65			0.64		

The findings suggest that RTM enabled GPD officials to make decisions about where to allocate resources *and* what to do when they got there. The intervention produced a statistically significant reduction of robbery throughout the target area while it was happening. In addition, the intervention produced a diffusion-of-benefits effect that was even greater than the reduction of crime experienced in the target area. Synthesizing results from above, it can be generally concluded that directed patrol had the greatest impact on reducing crime among all micro-level places in the target areas during the intervention period, whereas longer-term crime reduction benefits were best achieved via flyer distribution.

NEWARK

Newark is the largest city in the state of New Jersey, covering 26 square miles, with an estimated 2013 population of over 280,000 persons (U.S. Census Bureau). It has the largest municipal police force in the state. Newark has had a long history of endemic crime problems. However, the latter portion of the 1990s brought about a reduction in violence, mirroring the experience of many U.S. cities at the time. The tide seemingly turned again in the new millennium, with both murders and non-fatal shootings increasing every year from 2000 to 2006, according to police department figures. The Newark Police Department (NPD) adopted intelligence-led policing and reorganized many units to provide increased patrol coverage during evenings and weekends. The city simultaneously made large investments to upgrade many of its technological capabilities (Kennedy, Caplan, and Piza 2011). According to department figures, overall crime decreased 19 percent from 2006 through 2009, with murders and shootings decreasing 28 percent and 40 percent, respectively.

The city faced challenges in building on these successes in subsequent years due to a significant fiscal crisis leading to the termination of 13 percent (167 of 1,265) of NPD officers (Star Ledger 2010). This loss of officers, most of whom were early-career officers assigned to patrol operations, led the agency to phase out its large-scale hot spots policing projects, which had dedicated large numbers of officers to high-crime places on a continual basis (see e.g. Piza and O'Hara 2014, 713). In 2012, Newark's crime levels increased from the prior lows, with robberies and shooting up approximately 53 percent and 37 percent, respectively, over the 2006 figures.

Newark has a significant history of policing experimentation, most notably the Newark Foot Patrol study, which was initiated by the Police Foundation in 1978 and 1979. The Police Foundation reports showed that introducing foot patrols did not reduce crime rates but did significantly enhance citizens' perception of safety in the neighborhood. Citizen satisfaction increased, and there was a greater recognition of police officer presence (Police Foundation, 1981). However, more recent deployments of foot patrols in Newark have generated reductions of overall violent crime incidents (Piza and O'Hara 2014), suggesting that the efficiency of the tactic may have, for undetermined reasons, improved over the decades. Newark has also been the site of a number of research projects that have incorporated spatial analysis as a key element of the investigation of crime (Potchak, McGloin, and Zgoba 2002; Pizzaro and McGloin 2006). It has also been the focus of a number of research studies that have addressed different crime types (Kennedy, Caplan, and Piza 2011; Moreto, Piza, and Caplan 2014; Papachristos et al. 2015) and has incorporated innovative video surveillance and directed patrol strategies to address street-level crime and disorder (Piza et al. 2015).

FIGURE 12
Final risk terrain map of Newark.

Legend
Relative Risk Score
☐ 1–13.40 (<Mean)
▨ 13.41–36.00 (Mean to +1SD)
▰ 36.01–58.70 (+1SD to +2SD)
▰ 58.71–971.53 (+2SD to Max)

Newark, NJ
Gun Violence: 2012

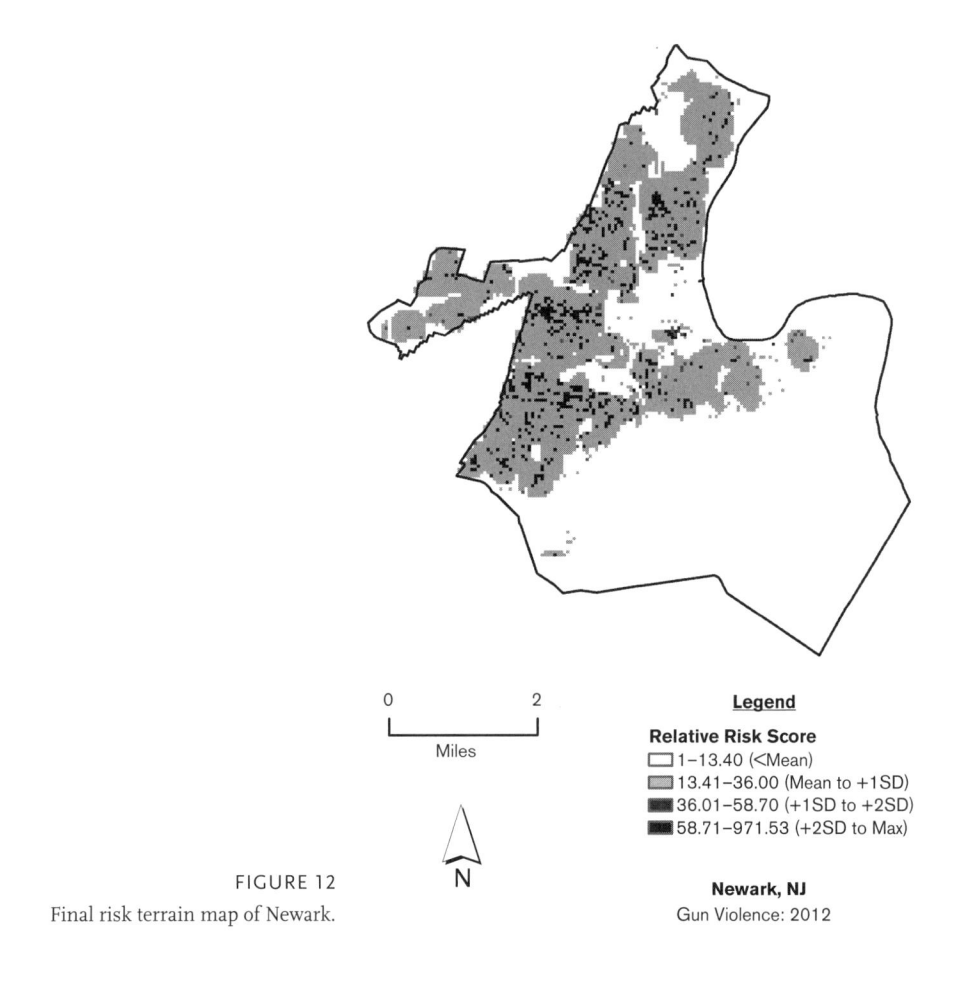

NPD identified gun violence as its priority crime for the risk-based policing initiative. Gun violence was considered as including homicide, aggravated assault, and robbery incidents in which the suspect used a firearm. The analysis began with a risk terrain model of gun violence in 2012. The spatial influences of 17 potential risk factors were tested: abandoned properties, bars, liquor stores, narcotics arrests (i.e., drug markets), parks, problem housing, convenience stores, food take-outs, parking garages, restaurants, gas stations, banquet rooms, foreclosure real estate, schools, pawn shops, Penn Station, and light rail stops. All geographic calculations were conducted using raster cells (i.e., units of analysis) of 226 feet and an average block length of 452 feet. There were 14,722 raster cells used in the analysis, of which 1,170 cells contained events.

A risk terrain model for gun violence was found that contains eleven risk factors: narcotics arrests (i.e., areas with high levels of drug-related calls-for-service, or drug markets) (RRV = 3.53), foreclosures (RRV = 3.36), restaurants (RRV = 2.76), gas stations (RRV = 2.54), convenience stores (RRV = 2.32), food take-outs (RRV = 2.19), bars (RRV = 2.01),

TABLE 18   Newark Significant Risk Factors

Risk factor	Operationalization	Spatial influence	Coefficient	Relative risk value
Narcotics arrests	Density	Half-block	1.26	3.53
Foreclosures	Proximity	2 blocks	1.21	3.36
Restaurants	Proximity	3 blocks	1.01	2.76
Gas stations	Proximity	Half-block	0.93	2.54
Convenience stores	Proximity	Half-block	0.84	2.32
Food take-outs	Proximity	Half-block	0.79	2.19
Bars	Proximity	Half-block	0.70	2.01
Abandoned properties	Proximity	3 blocks	0.36	1.43
Schools	Proximity	3 blocks	0.29	1.34
Problem housing	Proximity	1 block	0.29	1.34

abandoned properties (1.43), schools (RRV = 1.38), liquor stores (RRV = 1.34), and problem housing (RRV = 1.34) (table 18). Figure 12 displays a map of the final RTM in Newark.

NPD's risk-based intervention began November 13, 2013, and ended February 9, 2014. To reflect the RTM findings of the importance of commercial establishments for gun violence, NPD designed its intervention strategies to generate checks and manager contacts at three business types: restaurants, food take-outs, and gas stations. Each day during the intervention, a task force of three officers, under the supervision of a lieutenant, visited businesses in the target area. The officers were in possession of a business list with manager signature fields next to each business name. Upon visiting the business, officers were required to meet with the on-duty manager and have them sign the sheet, to ensure that proper contact was established. Given the nature of the intervention, with officers personally communicating with place managers in a high-risk environment, intervention effect was measured during the time period immediately following the intervention. We felt that the frequent contact with officers afforded the place managers a newfound method to report crimes to the police. This may have threatened the validity of the during-intervention crime measures. Our use of only the post-intervention period follows prior evaluations of police interventions that may have generated more opportunities for crime to be reported by citizens and/or discovered by police (e.g. Braga et al. 1999; Weisburd and Green 1995). For the current study, the post-intervention period of February 10 through May 11, 2014, was compared to the same time period from the previous year to control for seasonality.

Table 19 presents a fidelity check measuring whether the intervention activities were confined to the target area (figure 13). Approximately 97 percent (542 of 560) of intervention activities occurred in the target area. The approximately 3 percent of activities outside the target area occurred across seven street units in the catchment zones and eight

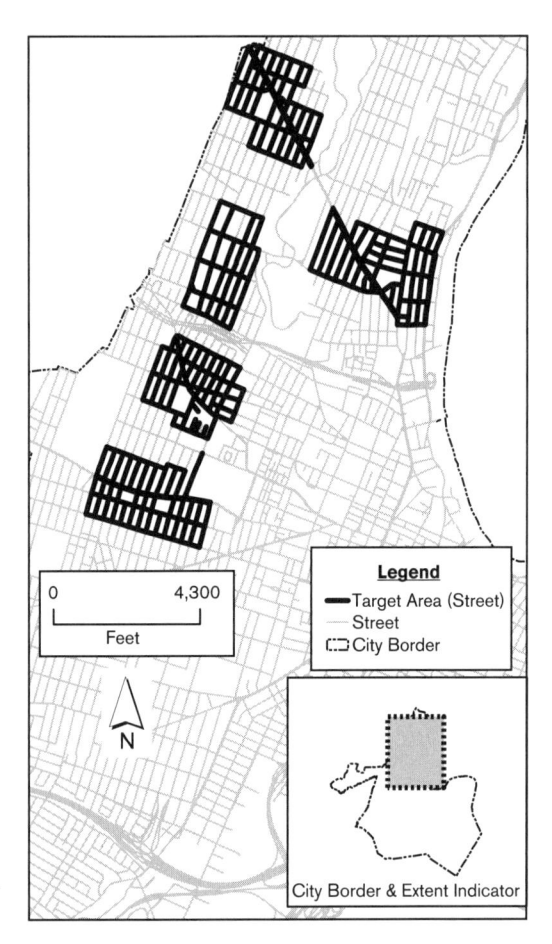

FIGURE 13
Newark Police Department risk-based intervention target area.

street units in prospective control areas. These fifteen catchment-zone street units were excluded from the analysis to prevent contamination of results.

Table 20 displays results of the macro-level (i.e., target-area-wide) analysis. Crime counts were reported for both the treatment and control areas. Treatment units were matched with control units via a 2 nearest neighbors PSM model with a caliper of 0.01. The results show a gun violence reduction of approximately 35 percent in the target area as compared to the control area during the three-month post-intervention period. There was also a diffusion of benefits to nearby places. According to the ATT findings in table 21, target-area street units experienced a crime count reduction that, on average, was greater than that experienced in the matched control unit(s). So, while the entirety of the target area experienced a statistically significant crime reduction, some places in the target area may have received greater impacts than others. The purpose of the micro-level analysis, presented in table 22, was to measure the effect of the NPD task force's business checks on the occurrence of gun violence. Model 2 reveals that the intervention

TABLE 19   NPD Intervention Actions, Fidelity Check

Type	In target area	Not in target area	Total
QOL summonses	1	2	3
Field interrogations	17	3	20
Business checks	509	4	513
Arrests	15	9	24
Total	542	18	560

NOTE: Eleven actions not in target area occurred across eight street units in prospective control areas. Seven actions not in target area occurred across seven street units in the catchment zone.

TABLE 20   NPD Macro-Level Crime Changes, Post-intervention

Group	Post	Pre – post	RES	Var(RES)	S.E.	WDQ	Phi
Treatment	42	51	1.54^	0.10	0.32	0.27	0.06
Control	57	45					
Catchment	53	47					
N *treatment*	177						
N *control*	180						

NOTE: PSM algorithm: 2 nearest neighbors, caliper = 0.01.
^$p < 0.10$

TABLE 21   NPD Average Treatment Effect on the Treated (ATT)

Crime	ATT	SE
Gun violence (post-intervention)	−0.21*	0.10

NOTE: Bootstrapped standard errors with 50 replications are provided.
*$p < 0.05$

activities were associated with a reduction of gun violence in the portions of the target area identified as high-risk in the risk terrain model.

The findings suggest that the NPD task force's intervention activities, which predominately involved meet-and-greets with business managers, are an effective approach to reducing gun violence. The strategy generated a statistically significant 35 percent reduction of gun violence in the target area as compared to the control area. In addition, the regression analysis found that the intervention activities were associated with decreased crime levels in high-risk portions of the target area. This suggests that future

TABLE 22 NPD Regression Models, Post-intervention Period

Dependent variable = crime change score

Covariate	Model 1: Overall activities			Model 2: High-risk activities		
	Coeff.	*S.E.*	p	*Coeff.*	*S.E.*	p
Treatment	−0.32	0.26	0.21	−0.33	−0.26	0.20
Total intervention activities	−0.03	0.04	0.37	−0.09	0.05	0.06
Pre-crime count	−7.93	1.17	0.00	−8.00	2.12	0.00
Segment	−0.06	0.25	0.83	0.04	0.25	0.86
Pscore	1.70	0.66	0.01	1.82	0.67	0.00
r^2	0.45			0.45		

NOTE: Ordered logistic regression model. Robust standard errors used in significant calculation.

replications of this approach should better focus officer attention on facilities located in high-risk places. The findings concur with prior research confirming that when police create active partnerships with place managers they can produce a level of guardianship sufficient to generate crime reductions in the vicinity of the facilities (Eck 2002; Mazerolle and Ransley 2006). It should also be noted that in Newark, a task force was established whereby the same police lieutenant oversaw the field operations each day over the three-month intervention period. Information and intelligence obtained from one day's actions informed the task force's next-day intervention activities and related decision-making. Unlike other cities in this multi-city research project, where different officers implemented one master intervention strategy and so the outcome evaluations strictly pertain to the actions performed, Newark's outcome evaluation was inherently an assessment of the use of a task force as well as the intervention actions performed by the task force. Ultimately, significant crime reductions can be achieved when a task force consistently and thoughtfully implements intervention activities at high-risk places.

KANSAS CITY

Kansas City is the largest city in the state of Missouri, with an estimated population of 459,787 according to the decennial census (U.S. Census Bureau 2010). The city encompasses approximately 318 square miles, spanning Jackson, Cass, Clay, and Platte Counties. The Kansas City Police Department (KCPD) is the agency tasked with protecting life and property while reducing fear and disorder in this jurisdiction. The Board of Police Commissioners governs more than 1,400 officers and 600 civilians, according to figures provided by KCPD. KCPD has played a key role in the development of evidence-based policing, with a number of seminal policing studies taking place in the city, including the Preventive Patrol Experiment (Kelling et al. 1974), the Kansas City Gun Experiment

Legend
Relative Risk Score
☐ 1–6.70 (<Mean)
▨ 6.71–26.70 (Mean to +1SD)
▮ 26.71–46.70 (+1SD to +2SD)
▮ 46.71–506.13 (+2SD to Max)

Kansas City, MO
Aggravated Violence: 2012

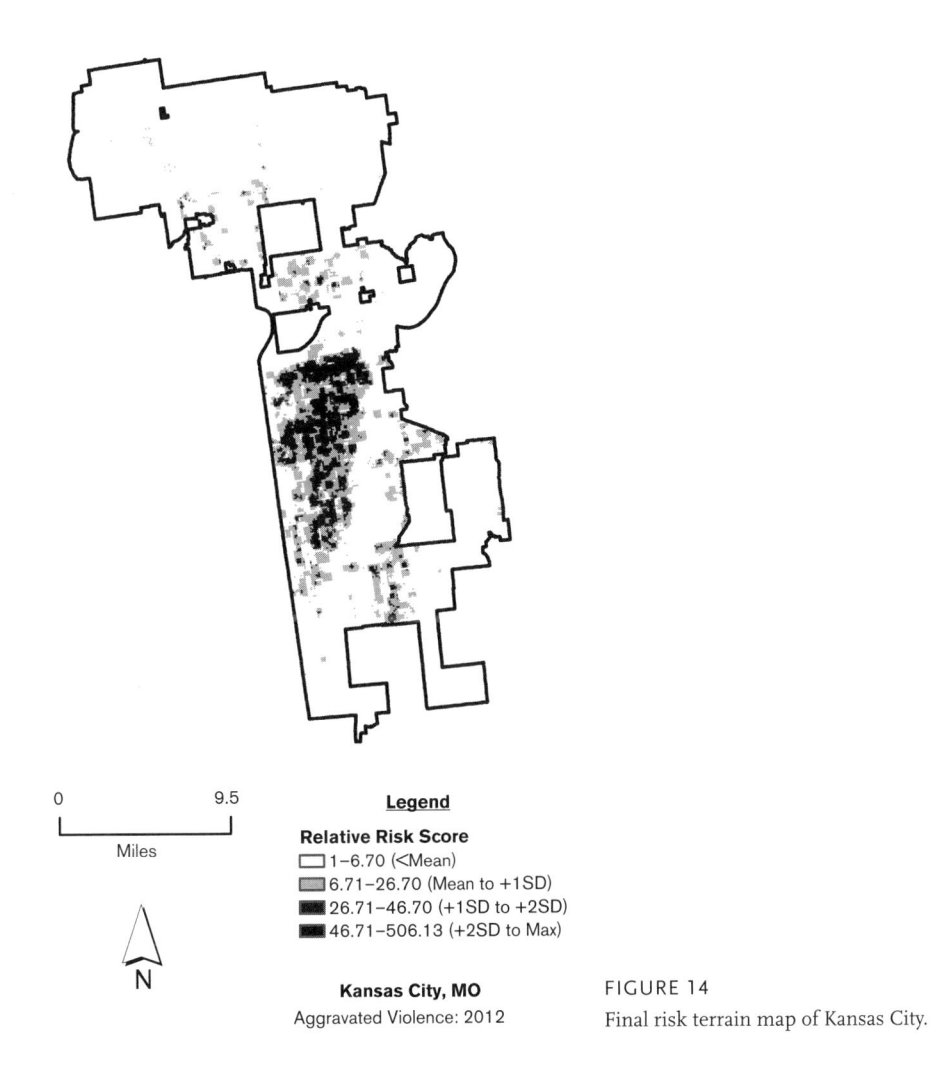

FIGURE 14
Final risk terrain map of Kansas City.

(Sherman and Rogan 1995), and the KCPD-led Response Time Analysis (Kansas City, Missouri, Police Department 1977).

KCPD identified aggravated violence as its priority crime for the risk-based policing initiative. Aggravated violence included all shooting incidents (hits and homicides), aggravated assault (with a firearm), and street robbery (with and without a weapon). The analysis began with a risk terrain model of aggravated violence in 2012. The spatial influences of 21 potential risk factors were tested: banks, bars, bus stops, convenience stores, drug markets, fast food restaurants, foreclosure real estate, gas stations with convenience stores, grocery stores, halls, hotels and motels, nightclubs, liquor licensed retailers, parks, pawn shops, restaurants, packaged liquor stores, schools, suspicious person with

TABLE 23 Kansas City Significant Risk Factors

Risk factor	Operationalization	Spatial influence	Coefficient	Relative risk value
Bus stops	Proximity	3 blocks	1.22	3.38
Weapon-offending parolees and probationers	Proximity	3 blocks	1.16	3.20
Suspicious person with weapon calls-for-service	Density	3 blocks	0.89	2.43
Variety stores	Proximity	1 block	0.82	2.28
Packaged liquor stores	Proximity	1 block	0.82	2.28
Hotels	Proximity	1 block	0.82	2.27
Fast food restaurants	Proximity	1 block	0.78	2.18
Drug markets	Density	2 blocks	0.75	2.11
Bars	Proximity	1 block	0.72	2.05
Halls	Proximity	2 blocks	0.47	1.61
Restaurants	Density	2 blocks	0.35	1.41
Convenience stores	Proximity	2 blocks	0.34	1.41
Grocery stores	Proximity	3 blocks	0.25	1.28
Foreclosures	Proximity	3 blocks	0.24	1.27
Liquor licensed retailers	Density	2 blocks	0.22	1.24

a weapon calls-for-service, variety stores, and weapon-offending parolees and probationers. All geographic calculations were conducted using raster cells (i.e., units of analysis) of 231 feet and an average block length of 462 feet. There were 42,814 raster cells used in the analysis, of which 2,152 cells contained events.

A risk terrain model for aggravated violence was found that contains fifteen risk factors: bus stops (RRV = 3.38), residences of weapon-offending parolees and probationers (RRV = 3.20), suspicious person with a weapon calls-for-service locations (RRV = 2.43), variety stores (RRV = 2.28), packaged liquor stores (RRV = 2.28), hotels (RRV = 2.27), fast food restaurants (RRV = 2.18), drug markets (RRV = 2.11), bars (RRV = 2.05), halls (RRV = 1.61), restaurants (RRV = 1.41), convenience stores (RRV = 1.41), grocery stores (RRV = 1.28), foreclosures (RRV = 1.27), and liquor licensed retailers (RRV = 1.24) (table 23). Figure 14 displays a map of the final RTM in Kansas City.

KCPD's risk-based intervention began April 13, 2014, and ended July 31, 2014. To reflect the RTM findings, KCPD designed its intervention strategies to address nightclubs, suspicious person with a weapon calls-for-service, weapon-offending parolees and probationers, drug sales, packaged liquor stores, and liquor licensed retailers.[5] An array of activities intended to mitigate the spatial influences of these risk factors, enhance community awareness, and deter motivated offenders were conducted by various KCPD

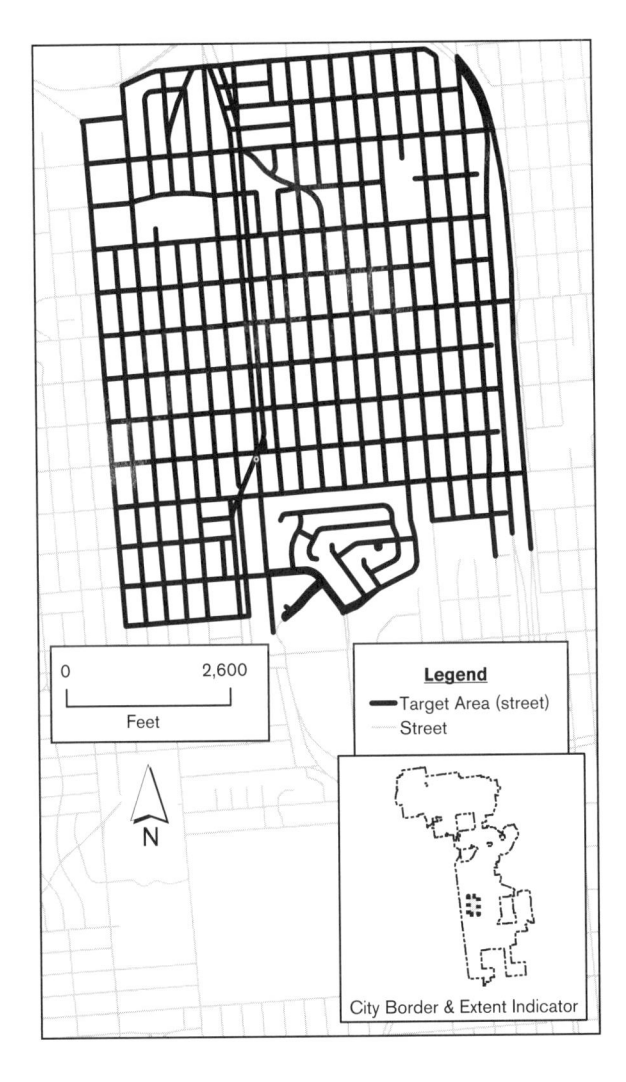

FIGURE 15
Kansas City Police Department risk-based intervention target area.

units and other city officials in the target area. The activities included code enforcement, directed patrols, licensing and inspection checks, meet-and-greets with known offenders juxtaposed with social service referrals/support, CPTED inspections, pedestrian checks, area presence, residence checks, traffic enforcement, and building checks. A new protocol for dispatching officers to certain calls-for-service in high-risk areas was also enacted. We were interested in two different time frames for the evaluation: the 90-day intervention period (the time during which intervention activities were carried out) and the 90-day post-intervention period. Each period was compared to the same time period from the previous year to control for seasonality.

Table 24 presents a fidelity check measuring whether the intervention activities were confined to the target area (figure 15). Approximately 99 percent (726 of 735) of

TABLE 24   KCPD Intervention Activities Fidelity Check

Type	In target area	Not in target area	Total
Car checks	169	1	170
Building checks	11	0	11
Traffic violations	283	4	287
Residence checks	87	0	87
Area presence	133	4	137
Pedestrian checks	43	0	43
Total	726	9	735

NOTE: All nine actions not in target area occurred across four street units in the catchment zone.

TABLE 25   KCPD Macro-Level Crime Changes during Intervention

Group	During	Pre	RES	Var(RES)	S.E.
Treatment	60	35	0.85	0.09	0.30
Control	90	62			
N *treatment*	137				
N *control*	195				

NOTE: PSM algorithm: 2 nearest neighbors, caliper = 0.01

intervention activities occurred in the target area. The 1 percent of activities outside the target area occurred across four street units in the catchment zone. These four catchment-zone street units were excluded from the analysis to prevent contamination of results.

Table 25 displays the results of the macro-level (i.e., target-area-wide) analysis for the during-intervention period, and table 26 displays the results of the macro-level (i.e., target-area-wide) analysis for the post-intervention period. Table 27 displays the ATT findings. Crime counts were reported for both the treatment and control areas. Treatment units were matched with control units via a 2 nearest neighbors PSM model with a caliper of 0.01. Results show that aggravated violence decreased by 12 percent in the target area as compared to the control area. The purpose of the micro-level analyses presented in table 28 (during-intervention period) and table 29 (post-intervention period) was to measure the effect of the disaggregate intervention activities on the occurrence of aggravated violence. In the during-intervention analysis, pedestrian checks, area presence, and residence checks were each associated with lower levels of aggravated violence throughout the target area. In the post-intervention analysis, building checks conducted in high-risk areas were associated with reduced crime levels. This suggests that focusing

TABLE 26 KCPD Macro-Level Crime Changes, Post-intervention

Group	Post	Pre − post	RES	Var(RES)	S.E.
Treatment	48	52	1.14	0.08	0.29
Control	78	74			
Catchment	27	17			
N treatment	139				
N control	195				

NOTE: PSM algorithm: 2 nearest neighbors, caliper = 0.01.

TABLE 27 KCPD Average Treatment Effect on the Treated (ATT)

Crime	ATT	SE
Aggravated violence (during intervention)	0.06	0.11
Aggravated violence (post-intervention)	−0.02	0.11

NOTE: Bootstrapped standard errors with 50 replications are provided.

TABLE 28 KCPD Regression Models during Intervention Period

	Dependent variable = crime change score					
	Model 1: Overall activities			Model 2: High-risk activities		
Covariate	Coeff.	S.E.	p	Coeff.	S.E.	p
Treatment	0.46	0.24	0.05	0.20	0.21	0.35
Pedestrian checks	−0.88	0.37	0.02	−1.13	0.66	0.09
Area presence	−0.48	0.16	0.00	−0.21	0.14	0.15
Residence checks	−0.70	0.36	0.05	−0.14	0.38	0.72
Traffic violations	0.13	0.15	0.38	0.02	0.46	0.97
Building checks	0.03	0.49	0.95	−0.06	0.18	0.73
Car checks	−0.23	0.20	0.24	0.11	0.44	0.81
Pre-crime count	0.85	0.23	0.00	0.83	0.23	0.00
Segment	0.04	0.24	0.86	−0.02	0.22	0.91
Pscore	16.17	2.55	0.00	14.50	2.42	0.00
r^2	0.07			0.06		

NOTE: Ordered logistic regression model. Robust standard errors used in significant calculation.

TABLE 29   KCPD Regression Models, Post-intervention Period

	Model 1: Overall activities			Model 2: High-risk activities		
Covariate	Coeff.	S.E.	p	Coeff.	S.E.	p
Treatment	−0.19	0.24	0.42	−0.09	0.23	0.69
Pedestrian checks	0.30	0.74	0.68	−0.49	0.47	0.29
Area presence	0.10	0.19	0.60	−0.16	0.36	0.65
Residence checks	0.16	0.33	0.63	0.18	0.45	0.68
Traffic violations	0.00	0.14	0.99	0.05	0.28	0.87
Building checks	1.11	0.61	0.07	−1.64	0.41	0.00
Car checks	−0.21	0.22	0.34			
Pre-crime count	−4.82	0.76	0.00	−0.12	0.44	0.78
Segment	0.20	0.23	0.39	0.24	0.22	0.28
Pscore	6.12	3.12	0.05	5.97	2.94	0.04
r^2	0.33			0.33		

NOTE: Ordered logistic regression model. Robust standard errors used in significant calculation.

building checks in high-risk areas has a lagged but beneficial crime control effect that surfaces after the onset of this intervention activity.

The findings suggest that RTM enabled Kansas City police officials to make decisions about where to allocate resources *and* what to do when they got there to suppress crime in the short term and reduce crime occurrence over the long term. Intervention activities affect crime differently over varying times and places. Synthesizing results from above, it can be generally concluded that pedestrian checks, directed patrol, and knock-and-talks have the greatest impact on reducing crime among all micro-level places in the target areas when sustained, whereas longer-term crime reduction benefits at high-risk places are best achieved via building checks.

CONNECTING RISK ASSESSMENTS TO INTERVENTIONS

Malcolm Sparrow (2015) suggested that police strategies have been too narrowly focused on law enforcement at the expense of a broader mandate to address a wide range of social ills. He recommends a more focused approach to crime reduction. Spatial risk assessments to identify emerging crime trends take the police away from a crisis-management approach to one that focuses on the emergence of crime (McGloin, Sullivan, and Kennedy 2011). However, to be truly useful in the way that Sparrow suggests, we should be able to operationalize these assessments to strategies and activities that mitigate risks that can lead to crime. This requires a clear link between the analytical products of risk analysis

TABLE 30 Summary of Findings on Risk-Based Intervention

Crime type	Effective action	Immediate impact, during sustained engagement	Lasting (or lagged) impact, post-engagement	Reference/setting
Personal				
Guns/shootings	Business checks with manager contact		✓	Newark
	Dedicated police task force		✓	Newark
	Pedestrian checks	✓		Kansas City
	Police presence / directed patrol	✓	✓	Kansas City / Newark
	Residence checks	✓		Kansas City
	Building checks		✓	Kansas City
Aggravated assault	Pedestrian checks	✓		Kansas City
	Police presence	✓		Kansas City
	Residence checks	✓		Kansas City
	Building checks		✓	Kansas City
Street robbery	Pedestrian checks	✓		Kansas City
	Police presence	✓		Kansas City
	Residence checks	✓		Kansas City
	Building checks		✓	Kansas City
	Directed patrol	✓		Glendale
	Educational flyer distribution		✓	Glendale
Property				
Motor vehicle theft	Code enforcement / property inspections		✓	Colorado Springs

and intervention actions that are meant to effect change through tying them directly to policing and problem-solving at risky places.

In looking at risk-reducing interventions, we need to consider those that are sustainable, as well as effective. For these programs to be both, police agencies must rely on the expertise and innovative skills of officers, analysts, and other local stakeholders in developing programs that work and are resilient. When developing these types of initiatives, one must be mindful of the caveats that Greene (2014) presents about being overly reliant on statistical numbers at the expense of knowledge drawn from police experience and local culture (something very much related to managing uncertainty as well, discussed in part 1). Any risk reduction strategy will need to account for the ways in which police address the contexts in which they are operating, the history of their relationship with the community, directives from political leadership, and past experience with crime control efforts. We believe that the findings presented in this chapter from CSPD, GPD, NPD, and KCPD demonstrate that the use of RTM as an analytical tool, coupled with multifaceted partnerships and policing strategies, can achieve these goals in a sustainable manner. As displayed in table 30, specific activities focused at high-risk places generated positive crime control benefits both during and following risk-based interventions.

CONCLUSION

Our experiences in different cities demonstrate the effectiveness of risk-based policing for risk governance and crime prevention, and also its flexibility to adapt to the different needs and resources of police agencies. The desire to address particular crime types or to focus on particularly difficult risk factors can be accommodated by risk terrain modeling and its suite of tools and resources. Knowing the relative importance of factors that contribute to crime is only part of the equation when addressing crime problems. There need to be, as well, reliable procedures for identifying and targeting locations where crime is most likely to occur. As discussed in chapter 6, target-area selection methods must provide a focus for immediate actions but also anticipate areas where crime is likely to appear next based on knowledge of spatial vulnerabilities and exposures. In the next chapter we discuss procedural considerations for adopting risk-based policing and the challenges inherent in instituting new operational practices in police agencies, specifically when such endeavors involve implementing applied crime prevention strategies via researcher–practitioner partnerships.

NOTES

1. $RES = (ad)/(bc)$

where a is the number of pre-intervention crimes in the target area, b is the number of during-intervention crimes in the target area, c is the number of pre-intervention crimes in the control area, and d is the number of during-intervention crimes in the control area. $RES > 1$ indicates a desirable effect on crime in the target area relative to the control, while $RES < 1$ indicates an undesirable effect. The inverse of the RES gives the crime difference within the target area. For example, an RES of 1.42 implies that target-area crime decreased 30% relative to the control, since $1/1.42$ is 0.70 (Welsh and Farrington 2009a, 727).

2. The variance of the RES is often calculated as $VAR(RES) = 1/a + 1/b + 1/c + 1/d$ (Welsh and Farrington 2009b, 135). This estimation of variance is based on the assumption that the crime total follows a Poisson distribution. However, much research suggests that crime data are more accurately modeled according to a negative binomial distribution, which accounts for overdispersion (Higginson and Mazerolle 2014). Using the prior formula would underes-

timate the true variance of the data (438). Therefore, variance was calculated through an adapted formula that adds a parameter to control for overdispersion (Farrington et al. 2007; Higginson and Mazerolle 2014; Welsh and Farrington 2009b): VAR(RES) = $[[(0.008a) + 1.2]a]/a^2 + [[(0.0008b) + 1.2]b]/b^2 + [[(0.0008c) + 1.2]c]/c^2 + [[(0.0008d) + 1.2]d]/d^2$

Standard errors of VAR(RES) were used to calculate confidence intervals for the observed RES (Lipsey and Wilson 2001).

3. WDQ = $([Da/Ca] - [Db/Cb])/([Ra/Ca] - [Rb/Cb])$

where D, R, and C represent the displacement, response, and control areas, respectively, and b and a indicate the period before and after the intervention, respectively (Bowers and Johnson 2003). A negative value suggests displacement, while a positive value suggests a diffusion of crime-control benefits. The WDQ and associated phi coefficient (used to determine the applicability of the WDQ) were calculated in Ratcliffe and Breen's (2008) Spatial Evaluation of Police Tactics in Context (SEPTIC) tool.

4. See Kennedy, Caplan, and Piza (2015) for the full evaluation report.

5. "Packaged liquor stores" refer to businesses whose primary purpose is to sell liquor. "Liquor licensed retailers" are facilities that are in business to sell other items, but also sell liquor, such as convenience stores, grocery stores, etc.

8

FACILITATORS AND IMPEDIMENTS TO DESIGNING, IMPLEMENTING, AND EVALUATING RISK-BASED POLICING STRATEGIES

Insights from Completed Researcher–Practitioner Partnerships

> **KEY POINTS**
>
> - Researchers and practitioners need to engage in a co-learning approach when they partner in analysis that leads to policy and strategy implementation.
> - The success or failure of an intervention is largely determined by the project's change agents.
> - A planned change model of risk-based policing involves four phases: problem analysis, project design, project implementation, and project evaluation.

INTRODUCTION

We outlined case studies of successful risk-based policing in the previous chapter. These and the other efforts mentioned in the book demonstrate risk-based policing as a viable paradigm for public safety and crime prevention. However, we caution readers against taking the feasibility of the approach for granted. Each case study involved police agencies leveraging their internal resources and developing partnerships to design and implement

A version of this chapter was published in the *European Journal of Criminal Policy and Research* in 2018 (doi: 10.1007/s10610-017-9367-9).

targeted interventions. Irrespective of the evaluation findings, the ability of agencies to get a new strategy off the ground can be considered a success in itself. Research has shown that police organizations can be stubbornly resistant to change, with innovations not taking hold because of push-back from rank-and-file officers (Leigh, Read, and Tilley 1996; Read and Tilley 2000) or taking a much more simplistic form than originally envisioned (Braga and Weisburd 2006; Mastrofski 2006; Sparrow 2016). Indeed, we have seen similar themes emerge with risk-based policing. While many departments have been able to seamlessly adopt risk-based policing, others have struggled at various stages of implementation. Our understanding of the successes and challenges of our partnering agencies is informed by the body of literature on researcher–practitioner partnerships and program implementation, which is reviewed below.

RESEARCHER–PRACTITIONER PARTNERSHIPS

Secret, Abell, and Berline (2011) identify key models of researcher–practitioner partnerships. Of the identified models, they advocate the co-learning approach, noting that it enables mutually beneficial collaboration by affording both parties the opportunity to contribute to the project in a manner that best meets their needs. Such a co-learning approach has been exemplified by the increased use of the action research model in criminal justice (Lewin, 1947). In his discussions of action research, Kurt Lewin (1947, 202–03) proposes that "research that produces nothing but books will not suffice." Problem-solving collaborations between researchers and practitioners should involve two sides jointly contributing to problem identification, strategy development, and strategy implementation. The action research model has been embraced by the U.S. government (Mock, 2010) and is exemplified by the Department of Justice's commitment to programs such as Project Safe Neighborhoods and the National Institute of Justice funding a wide range of research partnerships, such as the risk-based policing programs that are the focus of this book. The emphasis on action research has greatly contributed to evidence-based policing by contributing to the knowledge base of "what works" in promoting public safety.

Despite these initiatives, a body of research suggests that the typical process of evidence generation, primarily led by academic scholars, can present challenges to strategy development (Papachristos 2011; Visher and Weisburd 1998; Sparrow 2011). A consistent theme in the literature is the inherent divide between academic researchers and the police agencies their work is meant to inform, with academics placing a premium on methodology and statistical analysis rather than the policy implications of the study (Buerger 2010). While such emphasis regularly produces high-quality science, it may not always translate into research that is policy relevant (Wellford 2009).

Despite such challenges, the practical utility of researcher–practitioner partnerships can be maximized when designed in a manner that is mutually beneficial for both parties (Braga 2010, 2016). There are many examples where policing has benefited from research collaborations (Braga 2010, 2016). Strategies such as hot spots policing (Sherman and Weisburd 1995), problem-oriented policing (Eck and Spelman 1987; Goldstein 1979, 1990), focused deterrence (Kennedy 1997), broken windows (Kelling and Coles 1996), and, particularly pertinent to the current chapter, risk-based policing (Caplan and Kennedy 2016) were originally conceived by academic scholars based on insights from scientific research. How these ideas are implemented, though, is dependent on a number of factors, none more important than the willingness of police agencies to adopt these strategies and devote resources to implementing and continuing them.

PLANNED CHANGE AND PROGRAM IMPLEMENTATION

In looking at the process of strategy development, we can turn to Welsh and Harris's (2016) conceptualization of planned change. They developed a seven-stage model for planned change: problem analysis; goal and objective creation; program design; action planning; program implementation; outcome evaluation; and reassessment and review. To Welsh and Harris the process of designing and implementing interventions is dynamic. It requires the work of multiple actors at each step. For example, problem analysis requires the collection and analysis of data from multiple sources, with results ideally being discussed, interpreted, and disseminated among a range of stakeholders. Program design and action planning require cooperation by numerous actors with responsibility for addressing different dimensions of a specific problem. Evaluation, reassessment, and review require personnel trained in sophisticated statistical data analysis and program evaluation techniques. In ideal circumstances, these persons also work to disseminate research findings and translate technical language into a form more accessible to practitioners.

We need to be aware that not all program implementations work. Ominously, these failures are often glossed over in the literature. For example, Scott (2010) noted that an unintended consequence of the popular SARA model (Eck and Spelman 1987) is that several distinct processes of implementation of problem-oriented policing are artificially conflated in the single "response" stage. As a result, the analysis does not accurately reflect the complexity of program implementation, as the original model for problem-oriented policing involved a number of phases that require careful individualized attention (Goldstein 1979, 1990). Such issues are not unique to policing, as evaluations of criminal justice programs as a whole rarely include information on the implementation process (Hagan 1989; Johnson, Tilley, and Bowers 2015; Klofas, Hipple, and McGarrell 2010). In response to these omissions, a body of knowledge has begun to emerge, highlighting common challenges to program implementation.

From a multifaceted process evaluation of failed experiments by the Center for Court Innovation and the Bureau of Justice Assistance, Cissner and Farole (2009) found that many of the projects were unable to establish clear data-collection processes at the outset of the project. Projects that included robust data-collection plans were able to easily designate project goals and objectives and readily measure progress toward these ends. However, such foresight was rare, as most of the programs reviewed by Cissner and

Farole emphasized getting the program up and running over establishing data-collection systems. Berman and Fox (2010) identified similar flaws in the St. Louis Police Department's Consent to Search program. This involved an innovative strategy in which police, in response to community referrals, would request parents' permission to search their homes when their (typically teenaged) children were suspected of being in possession of an illegal firearm. In exchange for the consent to search, police agreed not to make any arrest if they found an illegal firearm (or any other illegal contraband), emphasizing the seizure of guns over the arrest of offenders. Police supervisors in charge of this project focused their efforts on establishing partnerships with the community and creating legally sound consent forms. Unfortunately for the evaluators, data collection on program activities, outputs, and outcomes largely did not occur. This lack of data proved costly when the project managers were promoted to another assignment, as the newly appointed supervisor had little or no information regarding the procedural aspects of the project. As a consequence, the project took a much different form than intended, with the unit coming to emphasize arrests of offenders over seizing guns.

Welsh and Harris (2016) demonstrated how the success or failure of an intervention can be largely determined by the project's "change agents," the people responsible for coordinating, planning, developing, and implementing a new program. At the outset of a program, a change agent must first generate the necessary support for an agency to find a program promising enough to dedicate the time and resources necessary for its development. Change agents must then successfully identify and recruit the necessary stakeholders to the project. Given that relevant stakeholders may not have always see eye to eye, Cissner and Farole note that timing is important regarding stakeholder recruitment. For example, the Brooklyn Youthful Offender Domestic Violence Court did not engage defense attorneys during the planning stages, under the assumption that they would object to the program. This decision later backfired, as defense attorneys strongly advised their clients against entering the program due to their lack of familiarity with the specific terms of participation. Engaging clients too early can also be problematic. Cissner and Farole observed such a situation in Baltimore, where a community justice task force included too large a group for concrete planning activities to take place.

After the recruitment of stakeholders, Cissner and Farole found that ineffective and, in certain cases, nonexistent leadership was a common source of failure in the programs included in their evaluation. Selecting leadership can be complicated, especially in the case of multi-agency collaboration. In light of these concerns, programs may forestall making tough leadership decisions or bypass instituting formal leadership altogether. With such a leadership void, key program processes and procedures can fall through the cracks.

It is also the case that supervision of front-line staff, specifically in terms of the performance of mid-level managers and supervisors, is key to program implementation. Rengifo, Stemen, and Amidon (2017) noted that agency supervisors involved in the Kansas Offender Risk Reduction and Reentry Plan verbalized challenges to the need, feasibility, and success of the newly implemented program, sending a message to front-line participants that the newly developed strategy was not worthwhile. The important role that mid-level managers played in ensuring adherence to newly formed programs has also been observed in policing. In the Scottish Community Engagement Trial, front-line officers reported receiving a set of instructions from managers that provided minimal and/or incorrect information about the project's purpose and objectives. Other officers reported being told that the program was "nothing new," as the officers already acted in a procedurally just manner during traffic stops (MacQueen and Bradford 2016). In another example, the implementation of CompStat, a particularly heralded innovation in policing, also demonstrates the potential effect of mid-level managers. In their national study, Weisburd et al. (2003) found that CompStat reinforces the bureaucratic, paramilitary model of police organizations rather than fostering the development of new, innovative strategies. A follow-up study found that mid-level police managers rarely communicated the problem-solving activities of CompStat meetings to front-line officers (Willis, Mastrofski, and Weisburd 2007), which may help explain why bureaucratic adherence to traditional practices usurped the innovative strategy reforms CompStat was meant to promote.

Finally, it is also true that agency culture, specifically in terms of long-standing practices of the agency, can present challenges to policy-makers interested in starting new programs. Sparrow (2008) has argued that public service agencies tend to address problems through tool-based solutions whereby existing processes and strategies are leveraged, regardless of their "fit" with the problem at hand. He contrasts this method with a task-based approach, whereby the agency organizes activities around the specific problem that needs to be rectified, often requiring the creation of new processes that were not previously part of their "toolbox." He argues that the task-based approach is more effective, given its emphasis on designing operations for the explicit purpose of solving specific problems rather than fitting into the existing organizational structure of the agency. However, agency culture and preference for familiarity often cause stubborn adherence to tool-based approaches.

RISK-BASED POLICING PARTNERSHIPS

Now we extend our discussion to reflect on how seven of our research projects shed light on effective ways of conducting researcher–practitioner partnerships, as well as program implementation. Agencies in four of these seven projects effectively implemented risk-based policing in its entirety, carrying out each stage from problem analysis to program evaluation. These police departments, and their precise risk reduction activities and results, were discussed in depth in chapter 7: Colorado Springs, CO (CSPD), Glendale, AZ (GPD), Kansas City, MO (KCPD), and Newark, NJ (NPD). Three of the seven departments did not fully implement risk-based policing, experiencing implementation failure at one or more stages of the process. In an attempt to not negatively reflect upon these agencies, we anonymize their names, referring to them as PD-A, PD-B, and PD-C throughout the following discussion.

Our relationship with the agencies prior to the start of the projects varied from site to site. Crime analysts at three of the agencies (CSPD, GPD, PD-A) had previously conducted RTM analyses on behalf of their agencies. Two agencies directly partnered with us on research (KCPD, NPD), with results of RTM analyses reported in peer-reviewed journal articles (Caplan, Kennedy, and Baughman 2012; Kennedy, Caplan, and Piza 2011). At NPD, we also had direct connections to the police chief due to Piza's previous employment as a crime analyst with that agency. Our contact with PD-B similarly resulted from the agency's police chief knowing Piza from his prior work. In PD-C, we did not have any previous professional contact with the police agency. Rather, the agency's director of research and evaluation reached out to us to partner on a risk-based policing project.

In 2012, we secured a National Institute of Justice (NIJ) grant in response to the agency's solicitation, "Testing Geospatial Police Strategies and Exploring Their Relationship to Criminological Theories." This award funded risk-based policing partnerships with six of the seven aforementioned police departments. In 2013, we partnered with PD-C on a follow-up project funded as part of NIJ's "Testing Geospatial Predictive Policing Strategies" program. This project sought to replicate the six-city study, with an additional component added to the problem analysis. In addition to conducting an RTM analysis, this study aimed to determine how the effect of various police officer enforcement actions varied depending on whether the activity occurred within a high-risk area, as diagnosed by RTM. We (all the authors and PD-C) felt that the findings of this analysis would help refine the intervention strategy by emphasizing police tactics demonstrated to work best within high-risk places.

In considering these applied research projects, we were influenced by the planned change model of Welsh and Harris (2016), discussed above. Reflecting on our experiences, we simplified their seven-step model to four phases: problem analysis, project design, project implementation, and project evaluation.[1] In the next section, we discuss our experiences in each of these phases, focusing on factors that, in hindsight, seem to relate to the successful and unsuccessful implementations.

FINDINGS

PHASE 1: PROBLEM ANALYSIS

The first phase of each risk-based policing project involved RTM of various crime types in the jurisdiction, which was successfully conducted at each site. Our direct contact with crime analysts likely played a key role in the widespread success of the problem analysis. As noted by Kennedy, Caplan, and Piza (2011, 51–52), RTM requires access to more data than traditional geospatial techniques, such as kernel density mapping. The need to access, clean, and use such disparate data can present hardships in certain instances. Our close interaction with crime analysts, who are typically police employees whose duties revolve almost entirely around working with data (Shane 2007), offered the precise data sets necessary to seamlessly conduct the RTM analyses. It should also be noted that the use of a researcher–practitioner partnership likely played a role in the successful completion of the problem analysis. Given the wide range of responsibilities that are typically assigned to crime analysts, it can sometimes be difficult for them to find sufficient time to conduct in-depth analysis for a new project (Brown 2010, 48). The involvement of our research team, and the fact that we handled the bulk of the problem analysis, likely reduced the burden on the crime analysts and made timely completion of the problem analysis more feasible.

Interestingly, the participation of a commercial partner also proved beneficial in terms of data access. One of the first steps of RTM is identifying a pool of potential risk factors for the crime in question through a variety of methods, including meta-analysis, literature review, professional experience, and practitioner knowledge (Caplan, Kennedy, and Miller 2011, 365). We emphasized the input of each police department's crime analysts and command staff in this process. In many cases, our discussions led to a great deal of brainstorming, resulting in the identification of risk factors that were not actively collected by the agency. As an example, NPD was interested in the effect of gas stations on gun violence, but had no internal mechanism for tracking such facilities because gas stations were licensed by the state rather than the city. In such cases, we were able to obtain the data from InfoGroup, a leading provider of residential and commercial data for reference, research, and marketing purposes.[2]

While the RTM analyses were seamlessly conducted in each instance, in PD-C we experienced difficulty with the second component of the problem analysis, which sought to measure how the effect of police activities differed across spatial contexts. PD-C was able to readily provide data for traditional enforcement actions, such as arrests, summonses, and pedestrian stops, as these incidents were routinely captured in their internal data systems. However, the command staff was adamant that these actions did not fully reflect their crime prevention mission, with focused activities such as directed automobile patrols, foot patrols, and team-policing units being emphasized by the new leadership. The leadership was more concerned with officers providing conspicuous presence at high-crime places through these tactics rather than with whether or not they took enforcement actions while on duty. Unfortunately, PD-C had no established means for collecting such data. Since any analysis that did not include such activities would lack content validity, PD-C opted against conducting the second portion of the problem analysis.

To be clear, this lack of data should not be considered a failure of PD-C, as modern records management systems primarily house data on official enforcement actions conducted by police. However, recent scholarship has advanced the notion that police could prevent crime by de-emphasizing formal enforcement in favor of conspicuous presence and more informal community engagement (Ariel, Weinborn, Sherman 2016; Caplan and Kennedy 2016; Nagin, Solow, and Lum 2015). Given the interest in such officer actions, police should strive to create processes to more readily reflect these less invasive activities. For example, Piza (forthcoming) measured informal "guardian actions" (business checks, citizen contacts, bus checks, and taxi inspections) from after-action reports submitted by patrol officers at the end of each shift. To measure general police presence, rather than police enforcement, Ariel and Partridge (2016) used GPS devices to track officer movement across high-crime bus stops. And KCPD's business checks, conducted as part of our NIJ experiment, showed the greatest long-term impact on reducing violent crime. Recording these activities conveys not only what works, but also what to replicate in the future when similar problems arise. Integrating alternative data sources into analytical products is necessary for researchers to more readily measure non-enforcement police actions, and to give police the credit they deserve when success is achieved.

PHASE 2: PROJECT DESIGN

Following completion of the problem analysis, we conducted ACTION meetings with each agency to discuss the findings for the purpose of designing the risk-based intervention. In PD-A we were unable to advance to this stage due to an extremely high level of turnover at the agency. Our initial contact at PD-A was the supervisor of the Crime Analysis unit, who retired during the problem-analysis phase. After completion of the problem analysis, we spoke with the new Crime Analysis supervisor to describe the next steps of the project. However, this individual was soon transferred to another unit, requiring us to introduce yet another new supervisor to the project. During this time, the chief of police also retired before the agency was able to officially proceed from problem analysis to the project-design phase. This required the Crime Analysis unit to start over in securing support for the project from agency leadership. By the time the necessary support was secured, there was not enough time to realistically design, implement, and evaluate the intervention.

In five of the remaining six cities, our meetings with the police agencies occurred fairly seamlessly. ACTION meetings typically took place over a workday or two, with attendees including the research team, crime analysts, members of the police department's command staff, and representatives from any outside units that the department anticipated might play some a role in the intervention. In ACTION meetings, we followed presentations of the RTM findings with a discussion of the agency's perception of the findings and capacity to address the significant risk factors. In many instances, police articulated the mechanisms they believed generated the criminogenic spatial influence of the risk factors, often providing examples in support of their observations (both key aspects of Assessment and Connections in the ACTION agenda). This process was typified by an example from GPD, in which convenience stores were a significant risk factor for street robbery. When discussing the RTM findings among our own group of researchers in preparation for the ACTION meeting, we intuitively thought this was due to convenience stores acting as crime generators, with high numbers of pedestrians (i.e., potential victims) frequently traveling to and from the vicinity of the stores. However, a police officer provided a much different explanation, stating that many convenience stores placed automated kiosks in their businesses, where customers could dispose of old cellphones for cash. The officer felt that this provided offenders a way to earn fast cash for cellphones taken during robberies. The crime analysts were able to provide empirical support for this view, with cellphones being taken much more frequently in robberies near convenience stores than in robberies at other locations in the city.

As this illustrates, our discussion with police personnel during ACTION meetings helped shape everyone's understandings of the crime risk narratives at play and to identify risk factors that should be targeted in the intervention. Somewhat to our surprise, ACTION meetings also frequently led to very candid discussions regarding the scope of the agency's influence. Each agency was forthcoming in determining which risk factors they could readily affect as well as those they could not. For example, foreclosed properties were commonly identified as a particularly powerful risk factor. In each instance, police leadership stated that addressing the spatial influence of foreclosures was beyond the reach of their agency. Thus, foreclosures (distinct from vacant properties) were not often a targeted risk factor in the policing interventions.

At PD-C, the project-design phase did not proceed successfully. The problem was not a lack of ability to meet with command-staff representatives to discuss the project findings. Rather, the problem was the lack of a mechanism to move these discussions away from the problem-analysis findings and toward the development of an applied intervention. This may have been at least partially due to the piecemeal fashion by which PD-C decided to approach the project design. Rather than hold one meeting with all involved parties present, as the other agencies did, PD-C held a series of separate meetings with different agency representatives, with long periods of time in between. As is natural in applied research, the research team commonly had to convince at least certain members of the agency that the project would be beneficial. Indeed, we had to do some version of this with each of the partnering agencies during the early stages of the projects. However, the unique meeting structure at PD-C complicated this process. Each meeting with a new group of stakeholders put pressure on the research team to "sell" the project as worthwhile. Even after securing the necessary initial support for the project and receiving federal grant funding for it, the multiple-meeting format hindered the project design. At the different meetings, attendees emphasized different risk factors for intervention. Also, as occurred in a number of the other cities, questions posed by officers led the research team to conduct follow-up analyses to clarify and build on key points of the RTM analysis, which informed the intervention. However, at PD-C, the disparate meetings meant that these follow-up analyses were highly varied in nature and did not collectively speak to any overarching themes. There was no institutional memory from one meeting to the next. Therefore, while the supplemental analyses satisfied the curiosity of the requesting parties, these analyses did not ultimately have much practical value for the project.

In contemplating the lack of successful project design in PD-C, we noted the differing relationship we had with them compared to the other project partners. Many of the departments involved in the original six-city study had some level of experience with RTM and/or a previous working relationship with the authors. In contrast, PD-C worked with RTM and the authors for the first time on this project. This unfamiliarity may have hindered our ability to move the project from problem analysis to program design. It should also be noted that our contact in this agency was with the Office of Research and Evaluation, not with any crime analysis personnel as in the other cities. This office was staffed with primarily civilian personnel, including the director. While crime analysts are also primarily civilians, they are involved in the day-to-day functions of policing, contributing the analytical products necessary for a range of contemporary strategies (Santos, 2014). The Office of Research and Evaluation, on the other hand, was primarily involved in more macro-level projects focused on overarching policy that did not overlap directly with daily police functions. Therefore, this office may have lacked the working relationship with sworn personnel to effectively generate support for the project.

Lastly, PD-C did experience some turnover, albeit not near the level of PD-A discussed earlier, that may have negatively impacted the project. In about the sixth month of the project, the director of research and evaluation, who had initiated the project, left the agency. A replacement was not hired for several months. From there, it took another few months for us to establish reliable contact with the new office commanders, brief them about the project, garner their support, and reconduct the RTM analysis (to account for the adjusted "pre-intervention" time period). This obviously affected the timeline for the intervention, as the problem-analysis phase lasted about three times longer than anticipated. It also shifted the tone of the project from one that was conceived by personnel in the police agency, who then solicited our support as partners for grant-funded research, to one that was all but forgotten internally due to personnel turnover, but that we suddenly had to resolicit as an agency partner due to grant-funded obligations. This new researcher–practitioner courtship was hampered by operating outside the police agency and without the well-established relationships we once had.

The effect that this had on the design of the intervention was less clear. During the preparation of the grant application, the original director committed the agency to participating in the intervention portion of the project. However, the new director, upon assuming this job, stated that field operations were well outside the scope of the Research and Evaluation Office and did not similarly commit to the intervention. Instead, the new director offered us the opportunity to garner support from the agency personnel responsible for patrol operations. In our view, the result of the lack of verbal commitment from the research director gave the appearance to the operations unit that we (the research team) were outside academics requesting support for our own pet project rather than members of an existing partnership actively funded by NIJ. This was likely damaging, as new (specifically innovative) projects, not previously attempted by the agency, can gravely suffer if no clear "champion" emerges from inside the host agency (Bowers and Johnson 2010). However, we acknowledge that it is difficult to determine precisely how much this contributed to the project's failure.

PHASE 3: PROJECT IMPLEMENTATION

The individualized results of RTM analysis at each project site, coupled with each agency's unique mission and organizational structure, resulted in applied interventions that greatly differed in scope, as discussed in chapter 7. As each city deployed its risk-based intervention, it was interesting to note the different management structures necessary for implementation. In certain cases, the focused scope of the intervention involved a small number of participants that seemed to facilitate management. For example, NPD's effort, comprising a single four-person task force, was managed directly out of the chief of police's office. The same lieutenant led the task force each tour of duty to ensure consistency in treatment delivery. Officers were selected for the task force on an overtime basis, with those interested in the assignment notifying the chief's office in writing. The pool of interested officers participated in the task force on a rotating basis. From our perspective, the NPD was able to manage this program with a minimal amount of hardship due to clear identification of a project leader (the lieutenant) and a relatively small number of officers to select from and supervise. Prior research supports this view, as projects requiring the coordination of multiple entities from different units are typically at higher risk of implementation failure than less complicated projects (Bowers and Johnson 2010).

Each of the other agencies designed interventions that involved a wider array of personnel from a number of different units. In certain cases, the management of the program was somewhat simplified by the designation of street segments encompassed within a single precinct as the target area, which meant that a police supervisor (typically a captain or major) was already in charge of operations in the area. This was the case with the KCPD, which selected the Metro division to receive the risk-based intervention. This meant that the commanders directly had at their disposal personnel to address the targeted risk factors through a combination of patrol, investigation, and code-enforcement activities.

In contrast, the designation of the Sand Creek division as the target area in Colorado Springs did not seem to simplify project management significantly. Comparing CSPD to KCPD, this may have been due to the different number of risk factors targeted by the respective interventions. KCPD sought to mitigate the spatial influence of seven separate risk factors. This likely maximized opportunity for multiple entities in the precinct to contribute to the intervention. CSPD's intervention was solely focused on social disorder, a top risk factor identified in the RTM. Given this singular focus, the Sand Creek commanders were challenged with leveraging all available resources that related to this precise issue. Resources were pulled from various units in CSPD, as valuable tools to combat social disorder resided outside the Sand Creek division. In addition to the patrol officers and detectives from Sand Creek, CSPD's intervention included the community outreach unit, the major crimes investigative unit, the city's code enforcement unit, and the city's sanitation department. From our vantage point, this required much more managerial effort than the interventions involving only resources from a single command or precinct. Nonetheless, the project was effectively managed, with the disparate entities holistically contributing to the intervention at each phase of the project.

GPD's risk-based intervention was heavily patrol focused, with patrol officers expected to carry out the bulk of the project strategies. Rather than focus intervention strategies within a single patrol division (the approach taken by CSPD and KCPD), GPD selected clusters of high-risk street segments in the southeastern portion of the city for intervention. The NPD similarly focused the intervention at micro-units spread across the city and successfully ensured treatment integrity, as officer activity did not stray from the target areas. GPD was not able to ensure that intervention activities were confined to the target areas. Approximately 9 percent (175 of 1850) of activities occurred outside the target area, with 59 prospective control street segments being exposed to intervention activities. This led us to reconfigure our original research design, with each street segment that experienced at least one intervention action as the "target areas" for the evaluation rather than the street segments originally selected to comprise the target area.

In hindsight, we cannot concretely state why GPD was the only agency to struggle with keeping intervention activities confined to the originally identified target area. Patrol officers on the whole were briefed on the project and instructed to conduct intervention activities when in the geographic target area. It is possible that the lack of an individual set of supervisors to ensure daily treatment fidelity led officers to become overzealous in choosing where to conduct intervention activities. Prior research has suggested that individual police officers often stray from predetermined intervention boundaries to seek out additional problems to rectify (Sorg et al., 2014). Risk-based policing may be particularly susceptible to such a mindset if target-area boundaries are selected without input from patrol officers and the importance of adhering to boundaries is not clearly explained by supervisors (Sorg et al., 2014). In contrast, NPD's intervention included officers under the supervision of a lieutenant at all times. Armed with a list of pre-identified businesses to visit, the lieutenant may have been better positioned to ensure that officer activity was constrained to the target areas than GPD supervisors, who were somewhat detached from the daily patrol activity.

Like CSPD, PD-B focused on a single risk factor (problem buildings). However, rather than design a completely new intervention, they used the RTM findings to inform an ongoing intervention. PD-B bolstered this effort by creating a computerized dashboard that notified building inspectors of newly designated problem buildings present in high-risk areas, as diagnosed by RTM. These buildings would become the new focus of the intervention efforts. From a program-design perspective, PD-B was able to focus its attention fully on the creation of the problem-buildings dashboard and training personnel in its use given the pre-existing building inspection program.

PHASE 4: PROJECT EVALUATION

Evaluation required that the research team be provided with the necessary data to conduct the analysis. At a minimum, we needed data on program outcomes (i.e., the crime of interest) and outputs (i.e., the activities that occurred as part of the intervention). Each of the five agencies that successfully implemented an intervention was able to provide accurate outcome data due to their use of a modern records management system. Records management also played a role in the measurement of outputs, as traditional officer enforcement activities, such as arrests and citations, are readily captured in these databases. However, the vast array of activities incorporated in the risk-based policing strategies meant that officers often conducted activities that were not so easily captured. Therefore, measuring officer outputs required additional effort on the part of the police agencies. For example, the aforementioned business manager sign-in sheets used by NPD each tour of duty were provided to the research team for digitizing and geocoding for the evaluation. In contrast, GPD tracked patrol officer flyer distribution by creating a new code in their computer-aided dispatch system to reflect this specific type of activity. Each time an officer interacted with a community member during flyer distribution, he/she would radio dispatch to create a new assignment reflecting this activity. This made flyer distribution as measurable as the more traditional officer actions typically captured in data systems.

CSPD was able to provide incident-specific data for each intervention activity except the license plate recognition (LPR) deployment. We were told that LPR units were deployed each day of the intervention period within the target area. However, no information was provided on the locations, times, or number of stolen motor vehicles detected by LPR. Similar to our observations regarding PD-C, the use of additional data technologies could have positively affected CSPD's analysis efforts. Had patrol units been equipped with automated vehicle locator devices, researchers could have readily identified the precise places LPR units traveled through each day. Nonetheless, CSPD did not experience any data-collection difficulties with any of their other project outputs, despite the impressive array of activities and units involved. Given that these other activities were emphasized in the intervention more than the LPRs, we were confident that the bulk of CSPD's output activity was captured.

Unfortunately, PD-B was unable to provide output data in a usable format, which prevented us from conducting an evaluation. We were only provided with the total counts of building inspections and summonses issued during the intervention. The precise dates, times, and locations of the outputs were unknown to us. The lack of location data was particularly problematic because the intervention target area was expected to take shape organically as the program progressed. Thus, we were not only unable to measure treatment fidelity but also unable to determine exactly where treatment was expected to be delivered in the first place. This may have been an effect of the overarching organizational culture of PD-B. With the appointment of a new chief in 2011, PD-B instituted a rigorous CompStat process alongside their pre-existing inter-agency crime-analysis meetings. As part of the weekly meetings, police commanders and representatives from other city agencies were required to provide counts of their unit's crime control actions. This reflects the limitations of tool-based strategy development (Sparrow, 2008), with the pre-existing agency tool (CompStat-style activity reports) insufficient for the task at hand (documenting risk-based policing outputs). To their credit, PD-B analysts contacted various parties at the mayor's office in an attempt to obtain the necessary detailed data, unfortunately to no avail. Looking back, having an analyst more involved in the day-to-day aspects of the intervention might have enabled better output measurement.

CONCLUSION

In this chapter, expanding on the analysis of specific interventions discussed in chapter 7, we presented an honest accounting of our partnerships with seven police agencies for the purpose of designing, deploying, and evaluating risk-based policing initiatives. We feel that this review points to a number of implications for the policing field. For one, our experiences suggest that crime analysts can be important drivers of innovative police practices. As mentioned previously, crime analysts were our primary contacts at most agencies. Crime analysts have long been considered valuable "translators" of research for police officers and commanders, communicating analysis findings in a manner more accessible to practitioners (Lum and Koper 2017). While crime analysts fulfilled this role in our risk-based policing projects, they were also oftentimes drivers of the project in their agencies. This suggests that crime analysts can potentially play a larger role in evidence-based policing than has traditionally been envisioned (Lum and Koper 2017; Piza and Feng 2017). Unfortunately, the role of crime analysts can be hindered by a police culture and organizational hierarchy that take little notice of civilian staff (Santos and Taylor 2014; Taylor, Kowalyk, and Boba 2007), given that crime analysts are primarily staffed by non-sworn personnel. Nonetheless, Keay and Kirby (2017) argue that the increased implementation of evidence-based policing can be an evolutionary step in firmly establishing crime analysts as true law enforcement professionals by making their work products central to effective police practice (also see Santos 2014). Therefore, expanded commitment to evidence-based policing may naturally lead to a situation where crime analysts play the type of active role that we witnessed in our projects. Piza and Feng (2017) recommend that researcher–practitioner partnerships embrace the knowledge-exchange feature of action research, which would directly expose crime analysts to the procedural aspects of rigorous research and evaluation. Ideally, this could lead to crime analysts "developing skills they can employ in their day-to-day duties" and allow them to "disseminate these newfound skills within her or his agency" (22). More directly involving crime analysts in the problem-analysis and project-evaluation stages of risk-based policing may help sustain such projects well after the conclusion of funding periods.

Our experiences in these NIJ projects also highlight the importance of localized versions of "tight coupling" in successfully implementing new strategies. The American criminal justice system is largely defined by the loosely coupled nature of its various components (Gibbs 1986; Hagan 1989), with tighter coupling often necessary to implement evidence-based practices (Klofas, Hipple, and McGarrell 2010; Welsh and Harris 2016). While the literature primarily discusses coupling as an inter-agency phenomenon, our experience suggests that this concept can be applied to individual agencies as well. Police agencies are comprised of various units and functions that oftentimes adhere to their own internal procedures, goals, and objectives, which may not easily translate to other units (Mastrofski and Willis 2010). Therefore, it is noteworthy that, in hindsight, most agencies appear to have focused the work of disparate units, such as patrol, investigations, and code enforcement, toward a singular goal. Indeed, outside of the NPD, all agencies leveraged the work of multiple internal units in addressing their identified risk factors and, ultimately, the occurrence of their priority crime. Police managers and supervisors closely involved in the risk-based interventions proved critical, as they were the people responsible for the day-to-day functions of the program.

Of course, the multi-pronged nature of the interventions was informed by the RTM analysis identifying multiple spatial risk factors for crime. In recognizing this fact, we feel that our experience has implications for data-collection activities of police departments. As mentioned earlier, many risk factors of interest were not contained in police department databases, leading us to purchase such data from InfoGroup. While the InfoGroup data allowed us to analyze the risk factors of interest, police may benefit from collecting such data on their own, especially when such data are inaccessible by third parties. For example, while pawn shops have been shown to put nearby residences at risk of burglary by providing easy opportunities for burglars to "fence" illegally obtained goods (Moreto, Piza, and Caplan 2014; Wright and Decker 1994), individual pawn shops may greatly differ in terms of the frequency at which they purchase stolen property (Comeau et al. 2011). Isolating such facilities may help increase the predictive capacity and practical utility of RTM. Therefore, we feel that police should place greater emphasis on the frequent collection of spatial risk data so that such information is as accessible as crime and officer-activity data, echoing the recommendations made by Kennedy, Caplan, and Piza (2011).

In conclusion, while we believe that this account of risk-based policing projects can be helpful for those interested in replicating this kind of work, the issues of program implementation did not come into focus for us until we moved toward the deployment phase of the initiatives. We originally did not plan on overtly measuring program implementation at the onset of these projects. While we realized the importance of this issue early on, and emphasized the documentation of relevant programmatic factors, we recommend that policing scholars rigorously document factors related to program implementation as part of *a priori* process evaluations. By doing so, practitioners will have access to the information necessary for successful replications of evidence-based programs (Johnson, Tilley, and Bowers 2015).

NOTES

1. In considering our experiences, we felt that multiple steps highlighted by Welsh and Harris were accomplished somewhat simultaneously at certain steps. For example, given the nature of the ACTION meetings, identifying goals and objectives, program design, and action planning operated concurrently. Thus, we decided to present these activities within a single "project design" phase in our study. Furthermore, Welsh and Harris conceptualized reassessment and review as the step during which evaluation results of pilot programs are used to make changes prior to full-scale implementation. Given the time constraints associated with the funding period for this project, we did not work with any agency on a full-scale, agency-wide implementation of risk-based policing. Therefore, we only include a discussion of our program-evaluation efforts.

2. See www.infogroupdatalicensing.com/why-infogroup-data-licensing/what-we-do and www.infogroupdatalicensing.com/why-infogroup-data-licensing/how-we-do-it.

9

THE ROLES OF MULTIPLE STAKEHOLDERS IN RISK-BASED POLICING
Case Studies of Jersey City and Atlantic City

KEY POINTS

- Partnerships between police and the community can be managed through regularly scheduled ACTION meetings.
- ACTION meetings with RTM overcome limitations of the "offender-centric" nature of CompStat.

INTRODUCTION

Working with police in Colorado Springs, Glendale, Newark, and Kansas City led us to consider how a broader range of governmental agencies could contribute to risk-based policing. All of these partnerships with police agencies devised strategies to mitigate the spatial influences of place-based risk factors. The scope of these interventions was commendable, as each police department incorporated a range of techniques expanding beyond traditional law enforcement activities. However, the range of possible intervention activities was limited to those that each police agency had the capacity to carry out on its own. This led us to consider the value added to crime prevention and risk reduction efforts from integrating multiple stakeholders, along with the police, in risk-based policing. By bringing more change agents to the table, we envisioned the possibility for agencies to focus on a wider range of risk factors and develop strategies that address risk factors in a more intensive manner. Such endeavors in Jersey City and Atlantic City begin to tell the story of such successful partnerships.

ACTION MEETINGS IN JERSEY CITY

An ACTION meeting in Jersey City, NJ (part of a U.S. Department of Justice Project Safe Neighborhoods initiative) exemplifies how risk-based policing can be used to problem-solve and develop multi-stakeholder risk reduction strategies. Upon review of the intervention planning intel report for violent crimes in the city, a conversation among those present quickly centered on gas stations, one of the top spatial risk factors identified by the risk terrain model. Police officers in the room quickly corroborated this finding by explaining that they had believed gas stations to be problematic for quite some time; now RTM confirmed their experienced gut feelings. Then a community stakeholder added to the conversation. She explained that many youth hang out after school near corner stores/bodegas where they can easily congregate and get food, drinks, and rolling paper to smoke at nearby vacant buildings. Bodegas close at 10 p.m., as required by city ordinance, but gas stations with food marts are exempted. These 24-hour-a-day/7-day-a-week gas stations provide space and "supplies" for youth to congregate late at night, creating a unique context for turf conflict, offending, or victimization. Bodegas and vacant buildings were also identified with RTM as top risk factors. So, a representative from the Department of Public Works added to the discussion, offering to prioritize existing efforts to board up vacant buildings and clean lots at places near bodegas and gas stations with food marts. Then representatives from the mayor's office and the Department of Parks and Recreation proposed enhancing their advertising and recruitment campaigns for summer recreation activities and job training programs. They would go to bodegas, gas stations, and places nearby to engage young people where they spend their time. Police commanders agreed to deploy directed patrols and business checks with managers at risky facilities, at peak time periods. Further, patrol officers were instructed to make referrals to partnering community agencies and social workers when people appeared in need of outreach or support services. A new protocol for crime incident reporting was also developed to help with continued risk assessments: officers were to inquire about possible connections among known risk factors and reported crime incidents, and to include standardized terminology in report narratives to enable queries in this regard.

This Jersey City account portrays how ACTION meetings permit stakeholders at all levels of a community to prioritize their efforts and coordinate responses. A key component of risk-based policing is to use existing resources (i.e., via reprioritizing or reallocating) so that even when external grant funding is not available, local governments can still employ strategies to mitigate risks and address crime problems at little to no additional cost.

RISK-BASED POLICING IN ATLANTIC CITY
BACKGROUND

With our colleague Grant Drawve, we initiated a partnership between the Rutgers University Center on Public Security and the Atlantic City Police Department (ACPD), the Atlantic County Prosecutor's Office, and the city of Atlantic City, to implement risk-based policing consistent with the techniques and procedures described in this book. It was a risk-governance approach that engaged ACPD with multiple community stakeholders. This now serves as a model for giving community members, elected officials, and police officers a point of departure from traditional ways of acting and thinking about public safety.

The initial goals of the Atlantic City partnership were to establish risk-governance practices that routinely inform decision-making and resource allocations that focus crime prevention and risk reduction efforts on places, not people. This was achieved with training on RTM, ACTION, and the three iterative steps of risk-based policing: assess risk; deploy resources; check for success. While Atlantic City and its police department had the technological capacity for extensive data collection and management, they initially lacked a robust framework for crime and intelligence analysis to aid decision-making for strategic and tactical policing operations. Atlantic City's wealth of "big data" required a structured and repeatable process for its analysis and review to become actionable by police officers in measured and transparent ways. This project sought to capitalize on and coordinate the various strengths of all public safety stakeholders throughout the city's overlapping local, regional, county, state, and federal law enforcement jurisdictions.

Atlantic City is 11 square miles of land off the coast of southern New Jersey in Atlantic County, where it is known as a tourist destination for its casinos, entertainment, boardwalk, and beach. The ACPD serves a local residential population of 39,415 (30 percent of whom are homeowners[1]) plus about 25 million visitors annually.[2] The visitor population creates a challenge for police, as many crimes in the city are committed by or against a group that is transient. While crime hot spots do exist in Atlantic City, a churning population of potential offenders precludes law enforcement's primary focus on *people* who may commit crimes, but is ideal for a focus on *place*. Being less than a few hours' drive from three of the largest cities in the United States (Washington, D.C., Philadelphia, and New York), along with Atlantic City's high volume of tourists and spectators at major high-profile events, makes certain places in Atlantic City destinations for illegal behavior. In addition to the day-to-day violent and property crimes, special events such as the Miss America pageant, triathlons, air shows, and beach concerts further subject the city to major public safety and security threats.[3] On top of this, like many police departments around the country, ACPD confronted a reduction of its sworn personnel by 37 percent from 2012 to 2016, leaving 271 full-time officers. This cut in human capital compelled ACPD to use technology, data, and human resources in efficient ways.

ACPD had never employed a crime analyst, which further impacted its capabilities for strategic planning and intelligence-led operations. The public's demands for improved safety (i.e., reducing both perceived and real threats) was difficult to satisfy or sustain without an institutional framework to routinely analyze data, evaluate intervention outcomes, or communicate policing efforts to various stakeholders and constituencies. In the absence of a crime analyst, problem definition is often based solely on officer intuition about crime characteristics, rather than systematic analysis; and policing is based on tradition and past practice, rather than evidence about what works best. It is worth noting that at the onset of ACPD's risk-based policing initiative, the department was heavily invested in making several information technology upgrades, including the implementation of new computer-aided dispatch and records management systems, integrated within a new real-time intelligence center to be located at ACPD headquarters. Risk-based policing offered a process for taking full advantage of these upgrades and for establishing data-driven approaches to policing in an agency whose patrol officers and commanders have long relied on individual experiences, traditions or "gut feelings" to make operational decisions.

The risk-based policing paradigm enables ACPD commanders not only to explain to patrol officers where to go because crime is likely to happen, but also to suggest why these places attract criminals and pose such great risks. Through the use of RTM and ACTION meetings, risk-based policing in Atlantic City was promoted to achieve significant crime reductions while taking the primary focus off people and putting it on places that persistently enable illegal behaviors. Continuous outcome and process evaluations are discussed in ACTION meetings to improve on past iterations of policing activities, fostering a responsive police department that adapts to dynamic crime problems.

THE PILOT PROJECT

The risk-based policing initiative began in Atlantic City with a one-year pilot project to establish broad buy-in, compile data sets, and test the predictive validity of RTM, as well as to optimize the protocols and methods for data management, data access, and information communication in the police department, specifically, and other city and county agencies, generally. ACPD's chief of police and command staff spearheaded the initiative, with support and consultation by our research partners and us. Progress began immediately with a campaign to establish buy-in among all levels of ACPD personnel and other city stakeholders, including city agency heads, business owners, faith-based leaders, and community groups. In sync with this effort to establish broad-based support, administrative data were collected to conduct analyses of robbery and shooting crimes, which were identified as the priority problems of interest for the pilot project.

Around January 1, 2016, risk terrain models were produced for robberies and shootings, using ACPD crime records obtained from the computer-aided dispatch and records management systems, city administrative data, and InfoGroup business address data. These data sets were representative of the full 2015 calendar year so as to forecast risky places for crime throughout 2016. The RTMDx software was used for this task. These

TABLE 31 Significant Risk Factors for Robbery in Atlantic City

Risk factor	Operationalization	Spatial influence (ft.)	Relative risk value
Bars	Density	154 (half-block)	5.1
Schools	Proximity	154	5.0
Hotels and rooming houses	Density	154	4.8
Convenience stores	Proximity	154	3.6
Parking lots	Density	154	3.4
Vacant properties	Density	154	2.3
Spa and massage parlors	Proximity	924	2.2
Retail clothing and accessories	Proximity	924	2.1
Laundromats	Density	462	2.0

analyses served as the basis for the pilot project to test the predictive validity of RTM in Atlantic City.

The significant environmental risk factors for robbery and shootings are shown in tables 31 and 32, respectively. Convenience stores, laundromats, vacant properties, and schools were selected as priority risk factors because they existed in both risk terrain models. High-risk places were displayed in risk terrain maps. The pilot project target areas were selected from among the highest-risk places for both crime types (by their overlap). They focused around just ten blocks, totaling less than 1 square mile. Police did not specifically intervene in the target areas during 2016. They operated as normal while the police chief and selected commanders monitored the locations of new crime incidents, sprees or high-profile events, and their spatial and situational connections to the designated target areas, other high-risk places, and spatial risk factors. Risk-based policing was little more than a tabletop exercise during the pilot project.

Early in 2017, in review of 2016 crime incidents, ACPD found that 26 percent of shootings and 53 percent of robberies occurred in the pilot project's designated target areas. Notably, the risk terrain model also identified convenience stores as a major attractor of robberies nearly a full year prior to the eventual fall 2016 spree of convenience store robberies. Citywide, the top 5 percent of high-risk places for robbery saw 48 percent of all robbery incidents (67 percent of all robberies were within half a block, or 154 feet), and the top 5 percent of high-risk places for shootings saw 26 percent of all shooting incidents (57 percent of all shootings were within half a block). The predictive accuracy of the risk terrain model exceeded expectations (based on these figures and subsequent empirical testing using the predictive accuracy index methodology described in chapter 6). This helped increase buy-in among (previously skeptical) police officers.

It became evident during the pilot project that, contrary to some perceptions among officers in the police department, crime moved around quite a bit through the city on a

TABLE 32 Significant Risk Factors for Shootings in Atlantic City

Risk factor	Operationalization	Spatial influence	Relative risk value
Laundromats	Density	154 feet (half-block)	5.0
Parolee residences	Density	154 feet	4.7
Vacant properties	Density	154 feet	4.5
Convenience stores	Proximity	770 feet	4.1
Schools	Proximity	924 feet	2.2

monthly, quarterly, and semi-annual basis. Notably, though, new crimes emerged at high-risk places, even when crimes had never occurred there before. Locations of robbery hot spots were the most stable over time. But 42 percent of shooting hot spots emerged in 2016 where they did not exist in 2015, and they shifted over smaller time intervals within the year. More than half (55 percent) of these new hot spot areas were predicted to be high-risk places according to the risk terrain model. Given these spatial-temporal dynamics of crime in Atlantic City, we learned that monthly RTM forecasts of high-risk places would be most accurate and useful for target-area selection. A risk assessment and resource deployment strategy for risk-based policing was developed based on these findings.

ACPD fully implemented risk-based policing with RTM citywide in 2017. Adequate protocols are now in place to support and sustain it as part of "normal" policing. Every month, RTM software identifies priority target areas and related spatial risk factors. Police patrols are deployed to these areas because they are forecast to be highest-risk for crime during the month. Police officers get maps showing the priority patrol areas specific to their district.[4] They also get instructions on what risky features to focus on, and what risk reduction actions to take at high-risk locations; this would have been decided at the regularly scheduled ACTION meetings. With risk-based policing, police still patrol all parts of the city, investigate crimes, and clear cases. They just give extra attention to the priority areas. Priority areas may shift over time as the spatial patterns of risk change. But ACPD uses RTM to anticipate displacement locations and stay ahead of emerging problems.

Police also use RTM to support various types of investigations. A burglary series in districts 1 and 2 that was identified by detectives and connected to a pair of suspects offers one example. Both suspects were arrested after a several-month-long investigation. Detectives had good reason to believe they got the right guys. But they also used RTM on the burglaries that were connected to these offenders to "geographically profile" their burglary location preferences. Cases that were already connected to the suspects had occurred in the high-risk places, as expected (i.e., their geographic modus operandi). But there was also an outlier burglary in district 5 that was located at a high-risk place. The investigation was reopened. As it turned out, one of the suspects regularly slept in a house nearby. So, now this burglary was connected to him, too.

One might ask why ACPD would not simply adopt the well-known CompStat process. Quite simply, there are several limitations of CompStat that the ACPD chief and the Atlantic County prosecutor did not wish to replicate, most of which were discussed in a previous chapter of this book.[5] Additionally, RTM—a key component of risk-based policing—is place-based, not person-focused; sustainable, with better measures of success and officer productivity; more actionable and predictive than hot spot mapping; proven and evidence-based; and constitutionally just (Ferguson 2012; Koss 2015). Risk-based policing with RTM and ACTION met the needs and desired goals of policing in Atlantic City; CompStat did not. There is no longer a sole dependency on traditional police performance measures such as citations, stops, or arrests, which demand offenses to happen first. New options for police productivity are added that give credit to whom it is most deserved when actions are taken to mitigate risks and crimes are prevented. By the end of 2017, violent crime was down by more than 35 percent in Atlantic City compared to the previous year, and this was achieved without increasing the number of arrests. ACPD truly focused on places, not people, to prevent crime. Police–community relations improved, too!

With broad public support, reliable and valid risk-assessment methods, comprehensive target-area selection and resource-deployment plans, reliable data-management procedures, and an established schedule for ACTION meetings, risk-based policing is highly successful, sustainable, and low-cost. It has proven to be a transparent alternative to "black box" data-driven policing because analytical inputs are vetted by many stakeholders; analytical products are distributed for comment at ACTION meetings; and well-informed community stakeholders enthusiastically support police to design risk-reduction strategies that prevent crime and enhance public safety. In Atlantic City, for instance, inputs and outputs of risk assessments are presented to all stakeholders at ACTION meetings to ensure that the analyses and proposed response activities will be acceptable in the context of police practices and community relations. All parties realized that their unique points of view have value toward achieving the shared goal of public safety. When police share the burden of public safety with community stakeholders, these people become partners to help solve existing crime problems and to identify and address emerging safety threats with activities that are effective, sustainable, and less susceptible to bias.

CONCLUSION

These accounts of risk-based policing in Jersey City and Atlantic City demonstrate how ACTION meetings have been proven to facilitate the delivery of up-to-date analytical products to key stakeholders that communicate ways in which crime problems occur in the jurisdiction and the factors that are important in lowering risks of them continuing. Data-driven evidence and professional practitioner insights are used to connect environmental factors and their spatial influences to illegal behaviors resulting in various types of crimes; to form risk narratives that help define the scope of intervention strategies; to specify procedures for implementing risk reduction activities; and to verify that these efforts work or else can be improved. RTM enables decision-makers to diagnose attractors of crime, forecast crime locations, develop interventions, and deploy resources. RTM with ACTION enables risk-based policing by multiple stakeholders that yields effective and sustainable problem-solving and risk governance.

NOTES

1. U.S. Census Bureau Quick Facts (2015 estimate), www.census.gov/quickfacts/table/PST045215/3402080,00.
2. www.atlanticcitynj.com/!userfiles/pdfs/Reports/ACVP08_summ.pdf, http://atlanticcitymaps.com/, www.visitnj.org/atlantic-city.
3. I.e., these events garner national interest and attract tens of thousands of people.
4. Risk maps and related information may be pushed out to officers in the field via hard-copy flyers, smartphones, tablets, dashboards or mobile data terminals.
5. For example, see Sparrow (2015); see also "Why RTM, not CompStat?" *The RTM Blog*, October 28, 2015 (www.riskterrainmodeling.com/blog/q-why-rtm-action-not-compstat).

10

PEOPLE MAKE RISK-BASED POLICING AND DATA ACTIONABLE

> **KEY POINTS**
> - Twenty-first-century police officers must come to appreciate how the data feedback loop affects their future work duties and related liabilities, and therefore, how risk-based policing is not only part of their agency mission, but also in their on-the-job self-interest.
> - Largely missing from the practice of public safety are deliberate investments in teaching police recruits the basic value of data and the operational utility of crime analysis for their personal and departmental interests.
> - A modest change toward normalizing data-driven decision-making would go a long way toward enabling risk-based policing to take hold in any police agency.

VALUING DATA: LESSONS LEARNED

Billions of public dollars are spent on real estate, buildings, and technologies to collect, manage, analyze, and communicate the many, many petabytes of data that police agencies generate. Fusion centers, real-time crime centers, CCTV and surveillance centers, mobile data terminals, and automatic vehicle location systems are just a few of the capital assets.

Each of these costs millions of dollars to build or set up, plus more to maintain and staff. Added to these appropriations are the costs of computer-aided dispatch, records management systems, and geographic information systems, to name a few of the digital resources, which comprise a multi-billion-dollar industry in the United States alone. Society values data and invests heavily in producing and preserving its related infrastructure. But there is a void in investment priorities: the human elements that make data analytics actionable for policing.

In roll-call rooms and patrol cars throughout America exists evidence that police officers undervalue data analysis. Or perhaps the value of data is just overlooked, and therefore underappreciated. Twenty-first-century police officers of all ranks have a symbiotic relationship with data and analytical products. Data informs strategies, tactics, and resource deployments every day. It aids criminal investigations, and is discoverable in courts of law. Data analysis informs policies, command decisions, and patrol activities that can directly affect officer safety, public safety, and police–community relations. Skilled analysts in many police departments throughout the country turn "big data" into "smart data," and when used wisely, these products offer insights to prevent crime and reduce risks. Police officers are both the generators of original data and the end users of crime analyses. Yet, they are rarely, if ever, formally trained to preserve the integrity of data measures, to see value in data sets, or to harness the full utility of analytical products. Largely missing from the practice of public safety are deliberate investments in teaching police recruits the basic value of data and the operational utility of crime analysis for their personal and departmental interests. A modest change toward normalizing data-driven decision-making would go a long way toward enabling risk-based policing to take hold in any police agency.

Basic law enforcement training programs in the United States last an average of 840 hours, or 21 weeks, according to a Bureau of Justice Statistics survey (Reaves 2016) of state and local academies. Major training areas include operations (an average of 213 hours per recruit); firearms, self-defense, and use of force (168 hours); self-improvement (89 hours); and legal education (86 hours). "Data utility" or "data analysis" is not mentioned. Adding an hour-long module to basic training would account for less than 0.5% of training time, but could yield a huge return on investment. Police are the front-line brokers of crime analysis results to operational practice. Yet their brokering skills and training are often un-nurtured and ad hoc. If policy-makers responsible for police academy curriculums add learning objectives to teach recruits why data is important, how it relates to their job, how it can be reliably collected, how it should inform their decision-making, how it can be used to develop crime prevention and risk reduction strategies, and how it can justly identify places for resource deployments, then police recruits will graduate with clear expectations of how they will produce and use data on the job and will better appreciate why commanders tell them to do what they are doing, and where to do it. Patrol officers will appreciate the transparency of knowing that data probably played a role in the strategies they were told to implement. Police commanders will confidently be able to explain the data analyses that affect their discretionary decisions and subsequent orders down the chain of command every shift. Twenty-first-century police officers must come to appreciate how the data feedback loop affects their future work duties and related liabilities, and therefore, how risk-based policing is not only part of their agency mission, but also in their on-the-job self-interest.

The raw data available to police only becomes actionable when people analyze and interpret it in meaningful ways. This takes training and practice; but it starts with an honest introduction. It requires a level of dedicated training similar to that already given to shooting accurately, driving emergency vehicles safety, or handcuffing quickly. Police leaders, elected officials, and many other stakeholders will realize long-term benefits when police recruits learn that data has value and how to harness it, and then when this permeates through the ranks as careers evolve and patrol officers are promoted. They will witness a more effective, responsive, and transparent police department when police officers are trained to balance empirical evidence with professional experience, and then to leverage both to make thoughtful, contextualized, data-driven decisions to reduce risks and prevent crimes. The mindset and operational practice of risk-based policing is stimulated by new generations of recruits who know to value data and empirical evidence, along with a healthy balance of critical professional insights and intuition. Police academies are the places to start to nurture this trend. Risk-based policing can be the incentive to start now.

BEYOND TRAINING AND INTO ACTIVE PROBLEM-SOLVING

Risk-based policing uses risk terrain modeling (RTM) to manage crime risks to prevent crime. It emphasizes problem-solving, evidence-based decision-making, and sustainability. RTM assesses spatial patterns of crime to diagnose environmental attractors of criminal behavior and make very accurate place-based forecasts, even if crime has not occurred there already. RTM is actionable spatial risk analysis that can be done easily with RTMDx software. Risk-based policing with RTM has been proven to work, with scientific experiments done in small and large municipalities throughout the United States. Research funded by the U.S. Department of Justice resulted in a lot fewer crimes where RTM was used to direct police patrols and implement risk reduction strategies. Violent crimes and property crimes are prevented because spatial risks are mitigated when police are deployed to high-risk areas. These priority areas may shift as the spatial patterns of risk change, but with RTM police are able to anticipate displacement and stay ahead of emerging problems. With risk-based policing, the focus is truly on places, not only people, to prevent crime.

You may already know where crimes are happening in your city. RTM helps identify *why* these places are chronic problems. *You* bring meaning and context to the analytical results via risk narratives. This allows policing operations to be enhanced, not replaced, by technology. With risk-based policing you get the credit for success and can replicate successful results over and over again. To more simply understand RTM, consider a place where children repeatedly play. If we focus only on the kids, we would miss the swings, slides, and open fields, that is, what we might define as a playground, that attract children to this location instead of other locations that lack such entertaining qualities. Features of a landscape are influencing and enabling playful behavior. With this in mind, RTM was developed at Rutgers University to identify the risks that come from features of a landscape and model how they co-locate to create unique behavior settings for crime—that is, to explain *why* certain areas have more crime than others. Many of us can probably imagine the clichéd "dark alley" when we think of crime victimization. In this case, we are considering at least two attributes of a landscape: an alleyway and poor lighting. We infer that the risk of crime is exceptionally high at places where these particular attributes co-exist. RTM does something similar, but in a more statistically robust way.

The raw outputs from RTM can immediately be used for problem-solving, planning, and police operations. For example, table 31 in chapter 9 presents the tabular output from a risk terrain model of robberies in Atlantic City. There is a lot of information and insights that can be gleaned from the results table alone. It communicates not only what factors are significant attractors of robbery but also which ones are not particularly important (by their omission). This can inform decisions to stop paying attention to factors that were once thought to be important, such as parks or housing projects, and focus attention on the spatial factors that truly correlate with criminal behavior but might have been overlooked, such as convenience stores or rooming houses. A relative risk value can be interpreted as the weights of risk factors. So, comparing relative risk across factors helps prioritize risky features for mitigation efforts.

We can also learn how risk factors influence behavior, and the spatial extent of this influence. For example, we might have assumed (through intuition) that parking lots relate to robbery incidents. But it is not proximity to parking lots themselves that heightens risk, it's areas with high concentrations of parking lots that attract robbery incidents, and therefore pose the risk of robbery. Schools might be given high priority for intervention activities since they are toward the top of the list with a high relative risk. But from the RTM output we know to focus on the area within a block from each school, as opposed to farther away. When our risk terrain model controls for time, we might find that schools are only a significant risk factor at certain times of the day (in the same way that bars could have a different spatial influence at nighttime hours compared to daytime, or weekends versus weekdays).

Risk terrain tables help make connections and shape risk narratives to develop risk reduction strategies. Risk terrain maps visually communicate the spatial vulnerabilities in a jurisdiction and show the high-risk places that will become target areas for police patrols and other risk reduction activities. With a diagnosis of the environmental attractors of illegal behaviors, RTM makes very accurate forecasts. In Atlantic City, for instance, police officers receive maps of the priority patrol areas in their district. Officers also get instructions on what risky features to focus on, and what risk reduction actions to take at the high-risk locations. Police still patrol all parts of the city and solve reported crimes. They just give extra attention to the risky places. Risk-based policing with RTM removes the need for a sole dependency on traditional performance measures and adds new options that give credit where it is most deserved. Police also use RTM to support various types of investigations.

We have conducted research on RTM in multiple cities across the United States, funded by a variety of agencies. Policing strategies targeted at high-risk places resulted in reductions of violent and property crimes as high as 42%, as well as many other positive outcomes in all the jurisdictions studied. Focusing on risky places, not only people, really works to reduce crime. We have presented several such cases in this book. We also found through our research that the environmental contexts for crimes vary across different cities and different crime types. This means that risk reduction strategies, and thus risk-based policing, may appear different across policing jurisdictions. Think about it through the analogy of a kaleidoscope, where the cylinder represents the particular environment, or municipality, where a risk-based policing initiative is underway. The shards of glass represent crime attractors, or features of that environment, such as bars, fast food restaurants, parks or grocery stores. Moving from jurisdiction to jurisdiction represents a turn of the kaleidoscope; so the pieces come together in different configurations, representing unique spatial and situational contexts that have implications for behavior at those places. It is well known that crimes cluster spatially, but it is not appropriate to assume that "standard" responses to crime problems at these locations will yield success. Behavior settings differ, and risk-based interventions need to be tailored accordingly.

Traditional analyses and responses to crime, such as density mapping and hot spots policing, assume that crime does not move—that it will always occur in the future where it did in the past, even when police intervene. A heavy reliance on crime incidents as the predictor of future crime occurrence is not sustainable when the goal of public safety is to have a measured impact on preventing crime altogether. Granted, it is very unlikely that any jurisdiction will be 100% successful at preventing crime. Unfortunately, what historically tends to happen is that crime hot spots remain stable or resilient over time, despite the many foot patrols, arrests, citations, and other traditional policing tactics used there. Hot spots tell you where crime is happening, but not why. Hot spots tell you where the problem is, but do not consider the spatial factors that make these areas opportunistic in the first place. Hot spots are signs and symptoms of environments that are highly suitable for crime, but they offer few insights for solutions to manage crime problems. RTM provides a spatial diagnosis. To stop playing whack-a-mole with crime we must realize that targeting crime problems requires a concerted effort to focus on the mechanisms that enable hot spots to emerge, persist, and desist over time. Police and other key stakeholders need to focus on the settings that influence illegal behavior. Risk-based policing is a framework to make this happen.

Police use RTM to problem-solve—to develop crime prevention and risk reduction strategies tailored to their jurisdictions. With a diagnosis of the environmental attractors of illegal behaviors, research proves that RTM makes very accurate forecasts of new crime locations. Forecasted areas become target areas for risk-based policing. And ACTION meetings become the forum for coordinated responses to mitigate these place-based risks commensurate with risk narratives that articulate the contexts of crimes at the target areas.

ACTION meetings guide the iterative nature of risk-based policing, with a focus on Assessment, Connections, Tasks, Interventions, Outcomes and Notifications. They include police and community stakeholders and can recur regularly to stay on top of the most pressing public safety issues. Crime risks are assessed, resources are deployed to the highest-risk places, and activities are recorded to check for success and reassess risks on the next go-round. Risk-based policing is essentially these three simple steps, with RTM informing decisions about what to focus on when police and other stakeholders deploy to high-risk places. When police share the burden of ensuring public safety with community stakeholders, these people become partners to help solve existing crime problems and to identify and address emerging public safety threats. This keeps police officers safer, too. And it goes a long way toward making police departments effective and their operations sustainable.

CONCLUSION

From RTM reports and risk narratives about spatial and situational contexts of crime, strategies for police and other stakeholders are developed that focus on risk reduction in order to reduce and prevent crimes. Risk reduction strategies are developed and planned by following the steps outlined in this book. What you should feel comfortable about by now is that making RTM results actionable is doable, even for beginners. At the most basic level, risk-based policing is a form of risk governance, which is very common in all forms of government and professional practice.

Risk-based policing with RTM keeps problem-solving efforts grounded and evidence-based. It enables better utilization of resources, with increased transparency for the actions of police and other stakeholders. And it is sustainable (financially, politically, and with regard to community relations). Legal scholars have endorsed RTM as respecting the constitutional protections of the Fourth Amendment while increasing objectivity and accountability in policing practices. With risk-based policing and RTM, crime goes down, and people get the credit they deserve for making this outcome happen. RTM identifies risky places and empowers police to think outside the box of the traditional person-oriented responses to crime. It puts the focus on places that persistently attract illegal behaviors regardless of who may be located there at any given moment.

The take-away from all of this is that it is important to consider the impact of the physical environment and how it influences crime outcomes resulting from human interactions at places. Risk-based policing with RTM provides actionable insights for improving coordination among various agencies and practitioners, for informing decisions about where to dedicate resources and direct strategies, and for justifying collaborative problem-solving among many ranks, divisions, and change agents. We all live our lives somewhere on the Earth's surface, so policing place-based risks makes sense, and evidence shows that it works.

This book has covered risk-based policing in the context of risk terrain modeling, risk reduction strategies, and ACTION meetings. These best practices enable you to focus on places to prevent crime; to develop spatial risk narratives that guide policing actions; to check potential biases in problem definitions, data or intervention strategies; to make data-driven decisions in transparent ways; and to balance the needs and expectations of law enforcement with the long-term goals of public safety. With these tools, policing can be proactively risk-based and not reactively crime-oriented.

EPILOGUE

I am a medical anthropologist-in-training. Before becoming interested in the emergence of "data-driven criminal justice" and "evidence-based criminology" in the United States, my research involved ethnographic studies of drug addiction treatment modalities in Russia. A central concern of this research was to understand how particular regimes of risk governance (e.g., recidivism risk management; HIV-transmission risk reduction) give rise to novel domains of scientific knowledge production and yield unique objects of intervention, and how these processes in turn engender emergent social, institutional, and political forms. These are core concerns within the field of critical medical anthropology, but studies addressing them within the discipline have been limited primarily (and understandably) to clinical, pharmaceutical, and biomedical research contexts, and among various medicalized groups. For my own part, I had grown so accustomed to the watchword "evidence-based" through my medical training (I am also earning my medical doctorate) that I could hardly appreciate the significance of such a curious phrase as "evidence-based policing" when I first encountered it.

Of course, as I have since learned, attempts to shape criminal justice policy with scientific expertise date back over a century in the United States. But still, there is undeniably something novel about the present confidence among many in the ability of better data and "smarter" technologies to help deliver on public demands for increased public safety and crime reduction while also redressing an increasingly salient crisis of police legitimacy, particularly in economically marginalized communities of color. Indeed, within contemporary political debates on criminal justice and policing reform, there is a growing consensus that in order to be both effective and legitimate, criminal justice in general, and policing in particular, must become evidence-based. The striking linkage here between the scientific/technical and the moral/political is what first captured my interest in researching the subject. When I pursued this motif in the literature, I found the bourgeoning field of "predictive policing" technologies. I was beginning to glimpse what I thought might be an important and timely investigation.

A survey of the scholarly and popular literature on predictive policing led me to think that risk terrain modeling (RTM) might be unique among these technologies. It wasn't so much the technical particulars that most interested me, or the statistical validity of its models, or the accuracy of its forecasts. What struck me was the slogan, "Places, not people," and what it seemed to capture about contemporary aspirations for better, more equitable policing through the technologically mediated construction of new objects of criminological knowledge and police intervention. When I contacted Joel Caplan about my interest in RTM as a case study for understanding how criminological research and theory were being translated into police practice, he agreed to meet with me the following week in Philadelphia. A couple weeks later, I traveled to Newark, where Joel introduced me to Les Kennedy.

In those early conversations, I learned that the creators of RTM had in mind something much more than a black-box computer program for making predictions about when and where crime was going to happen (they have always eschewed the "predictive policing" label). Instead, what they envisioned would entail wide-ranging institutional reconfigurations, both within policing organizations, and in relation to other agencies and the publics that they are mandated to serve. These changes, I learned, would in large part be enacted through an organizational innovation: the ACTION meeting.

As I see it, and I don't know that the authors of this book would entirely agree, the ACTION meeting is the principal technology (the word is used here in its broadest sense) of risk-based policing. RTM, understood strictly as the crime analysis and crime mapping methodology, can, but won't necessarily, provide the platform for risk-based policing. That is to say, a police agency could *use* RTM in their operations and still not be *doing* risk-based policing. As this book makes clear, many agencies have used RTM as a complement or supplement to their standard operations. In such cases, RTM is said to make resource allocation and deployment more efficient, and perhaps more transparent. But these are matters of degree. By contrast, the dual form of the ACTION meeting—police-only coupled with community-stakeholder—signals a qualitative shift in modes of knowledge production, both within police agencies and between police and their publics. The intended effect of ACTION meetings is to partially redistribute knowledge-making processes, making them more open-ended, participatory, and dialogic.

The metaphor of the *kaleidoscope* and the concept of *spatial influence* suggest that every risk terrain is singular and emergent, emanating from a multiplicity of local knowledges. In this sense, RTM cannot be understood as an inert, transposable technology. The virtual maps that RTM generates do not pretend to scientific objectivity in the absolute sense, but are instead construed as providing referents for intersubjective meaning-making and coordinates for collective action. The degree to which this ideal is actualized in practice depends upon the extent to which multiple and variously positioned actors participate in the terrain's rendering. After all, crime is a preeminently cultural phenomenon, an artifact of social practice (much like *place* itself). Hence the inherent problems with treating enforcement and reporting as "objective" measures of law-breaking itself, and why the very notion of an "objective science of crime" has always drawn scorn from anti-positivists. The ACTION meeting represents a pragmatic way to split the baby. The "risk" in risk terrain modeling, while a quantifiable metric, is understood in the subjectivist or Bayesian sense to be a function of (always partial) knowledge. Data-driven risk assessment offers a way to iteratively and reflexively guide socially coordinated action in an ever-evolving field. The relative and relational concept of risk displaces such binary absolutes as "opportunity" while still providing (at least ideally) a means of measuring the effects of interventions.

If this reading of the idealized ACTION meeting is on the mark, then risk-based policing would indeed entail much more significant transformations than a mere "new tool in the toolbox" interpretation would allow, and is therefore likely to run up against certain deep-seated challenges. For one, the profoundly asymmetrical power relations that internally structure a police department present a significant obstacle to the actualization of a truly participatory, decentralized process of knowledge production within the agency. The unanticipated consequences of CompStat should provide a cautionary tale for those who do not take this seriously. Beyond the problem of the differential valuation of knowledge based on position or rank, there are serious implications of the redistribution of liability attendant to practices that incentivize rank-and-file officers to take initiative or "think outside the box." After all, to compete for credit is also to take on greater individual risk. In such a high-stakes profession as policing, the repercussions of such competitive risk-taking can be severe. This, of course, bears on the seminal tension within the policing profession between officer discretion and the imperative to (re)act always within the constraints of the law. As police scholars have noted, proactive crime prevention necessarily requires some degree of discretionary preemption. But limiting such discretion is at the center of contemporary calls for greater accountability for individual officers.

These observations present very difficult questions, but so far we have only implicated the police-only ACTION meeting. The community-stakeholder ACTION meeting presents an even more fundamental reorganization of the boundary between police and public. As many have observed, the authority to unilaterally and nonnegotiably define a situation seems a defining feature of police. But in order to participate in the community-stakeholder ACTION meeting—if it is to be more than an empty pretense to procedural inclusion—police must admit the partial, and therefore fallible, nature of their knowledge. Here, rather than quash multivocality as a matter of course, police would positively valorize and encourage it. Police have long relied on the communities they police for information. This has been formalized through such forums as civic association or neighborhood watch meetings, or through the enrollment of paid informants. But the institutionalization of collaborative knowledge-making in ACTION meetings as mediated by RTM represents something new, inasmuch as the risk terrain emerges from a continual process of *co-authorship*. It is here that I see the most profound implications of a turn to risk-based policing.

Lee Young, MD-PhD candidate,
University of Pennsylvania

REFERENCES

Agnew, R. (2011). Crime and time: the temporal patterning of causal variables. *Theoretical Criminology* 15(2):115–40.

Allais, M. (1953). Le comportement de l'homme rationnel devant le risque: critique des postulats et axiomes de l'ecole americaine. *Econometrica* 21(4):503–46.

Andresen, M. (2014). *Environmental criminology: evolution, theory, and practice.* London: Routledge.

Apel, R., and Sweeten, G. (2010). Propensity score matching in criminology and criminal justice. In A. Piquero and D. Weisburd (eds.), *Handbook of quantitative criminology.* New York: Springer.

Ariel, B., and Partridge, H. (2016). Predictable policing: measuring the crime control benefits of hotspots policing at bus stops. *Journal of Quantitative Criminology* 33(4):809–33. doi: 10.1007/s10940-016-9312-y.

Ariel, B., Weinborn, C., and Sherman, L. (2016). "Soft" policing at hot spots: do police community support officers work? A randomized controlled trial. *Journal of Experimental Criminology* 12(3):277–317.

Austin, P., Grootendorst, P., and Anderson, G. (2007). A comparison of the ability of different propensity score models to balance measured variables between treated and untreated subjects: a Monte Carlo study. *Statistics in Medicine* 26:734–53.

Barnum, J. D., Caplan, J. M., Kennedy, L. W., and Piza, E. L. (2017). The crime kaleidoscope: a cross-jurisdictional analysis of place features and crime in three urban environments. *Applied Geography* 79:203–21.

Beck, U. (1992). *Risk society: towards a new modernity.* London: Sage.

Berman, G., & Fox, A. (2010). *Trial & error in criminal justice reform. Learning from failure.* Washington, DC: Urban Institute Press.

Bernasco, W., and Block, R. (2011). Robberies in Chicago: a block-level analysis of the influence of crime generators, crime attractors, and offender anchor points. *Journal of Research in Crime and Delinquency* 48(1):33–57.

Blackburn, B. (March 3, 2017). New research in Tarrant County targets abuse. WFAA 8 ABC. Retrieved from http://www.wfaa.com/article/news/new-research-in-tarrant-county-targets-abuse/419071412.

Block, R., and Block, C. R. (2004). Spatial and temporal analysis of crime (STAC). In N. Levine (ed.), *CrimeStat III: a spatial statistics program for the analysis of crime incident locations*, 7.1–7.18. Houston, TX: Ned Levine & Associates.

Bond, B. J., and Braga, A. (2013). Rethinking the Compstat process to enhance problem-solving responses: insights from a randomized field experiment. *Police Practice and Research* 16(1):22–35.

Bowers, K., & Johnson, S. (2010). Implementation failure and success: Some lessons from England. In J. Knutsson & R. Clarke (eds.), *Putting theory to work. Implementing situational prevention and problem- oriented policing.* Crime prevention studies (vol. 20, pp. 163–198). Boulder, CO: Lynne Rienner.

Bowers, K., and Johnson, S. (2003). Measuring the geographical displacement and diffusion of benefit effects of crime prevention activity. *Journal of Quantitative Criminology* 19:275–301.

Braga, A. (2010). Setting a higher standard for the evaluation of problem-oriented policing initiatives. *Criminology & Public Policy* 9(1):173–82.

Braga, A. (2015). *Crime and policing revisited.* Cambridge, MA: Harvard Kennedy School of Government, Program in Criminal Justice Policy and Management, Executive Session on Policing and Public Safety. Washington, DC: Office of Justice Programs, National Institute of Justice, US Department of Justice.

Braga, A. (2016). The value of "pracademics" in enhancing crime analysis in police departments. *Policing: A Journal of Policy and Practice* 10(3):308–14.

Braga, A., Flynn, E., Kelling, G., and Coles, C. (2011). *Moving the work of criminal investigators towards crime control.* New Perspectives in Policing. Harvard University Executive Session on Policing and Public Safety. Cambridge, MA: Harvard Kennedy School of Government, Program in Criminal Justice Policy and Management, Executive Session on Policing and Public Safety. Washington, DC: Office of Justice Programs, National Institute of Justice, US Department of Justice.

Braga, A., Papachristos, A., and Hureau, D. (2010). The concentration and stability of gun violence at micro places in Boston, 1980–2008. *Journal of Quantitative Criminology* 26:33–53.

Braga, A., Papachristos, A. & Hureau, D. (2014). The effects of hot spots policing on crime: an updated systematic review and meta-analysis. *Justice Quarterly*, 31(4), 633–663.

Braga, A., Papachristos, A., and Hureau, D. (2012) Hot spots policing effects on crime. *Campbell Systematic Reviews* 2012:8.

Braga, A., and Weisburd, D. (2006). Problem-oriented policing: the disconnect between principles and practice. In D. Weisburd and A. Braga (eds.), *Police innovation: contrasting perspectives*, 133–54. New York: Cambridge University Press.

Braga, A., Weisburd, D., Waring, E., Mazerolle, L., and Gajewski, F. (1999). Problem-oriented policing in violent crime places: a randomized controlled experiment. *Criminology* 37(3):541–80.

Braga, A., Welsh, B., and Schnell, C. (2015). Can policing disorder reduce crime? a systematic review and meta-analysis. *Journal of Research in Crime and Delinquency* 52(4):567–88.

Brantingham, P., and Brantingham, P. (1985). Criminality of place. *European Journal on Criminal Policy and Research* 3:5–26.

Brantingham, P., and Brantingham, P. (1993). Nodes, paths and edges: consideration on the complexity of crime and the physical environment. *Journal of Environmental Psychology* 13:32–28.

Brantingham, P., and Brantingham, P. (2008). Crime pattern theory. In R. Wortley and L. Mazerolle, *Environmental criminology and crime analysis*. New York: Routledge.

Bratton, W. and G. Kelling (2015) Why we need broken windows policing. *City Journal*. Winter.

Bratton, W., and Knobler, P. (1998). *Turnaround: how America's top cop reversed the crime epidemic*. New York: Random House.

Brown, R. (2010). The role of project management in implementing community safety initiatives. In J. Knutsson & R. Clarke (eds.), *Putting theory to work. Implementing situational prevention and problem-oriented policing*. Crime prevention studies (vol. 20, pp. 37–64). Boulder, CO: Lynne Rienner.

Buerger, M. (2010). Policing and research: two cultures separate by an almost-common languague. *Police Practice and Research* 11(2):135–43.

Buerger, M., and Mazerolle, L. (1998). Third-party policing: a theoretical analysis of an emerging trend. *Justice Quarterly* 15(2):301–27.

Burgess, E. W., and Park, R. (1921). *The city*. Chicago, IL: University of Chicago Press.

Bursik, R. (1988). Social disorganization and theories of crime and delinquency: problems and prospects. *Criminology* 26(4):519–51.

Caplan, J., and Kennedy, L. (2016). *Risk terrain modeling: crime prediction and risk reduction*. Oakland, CA: University of California Press.

Caplan, J., Kennedy, L., and Baughman, J. (2012). Kansas City's violent crime initiative: a place-based evaluation of location-specific intervention activites during a fixed time period. *Crime Mapping* 4(2):9–37.

Caplan, J., Kennedy, L., and Miller, J. (2011). Risk terrain modeling: brokering criminological theory and GIS methods for crime forecasting. *Justice Quarterly* 28(2): 360–81.

Caplan, J., Kennedy, L., and Piza, E. (2013). *Risk Terrain Modeling Diagnostics user manual* (version 1.0). Newark, NJ: Rutgers Center on Public Security.

Chainey, S., Thompson, L., and Uhlig, S. (2008). The utility of hotspot mapping for predicting spatial patterns of crime. *Security Journal* 21:4–28.

Cissner, A., and Farole, D. (2009). *Avoiding failures of implementation: lessons from process evaluations*. New York: Center for Court Innovation. Washington, DC: Bureau of Justice Assistance.

Clarke, R. V. (1998). Defining police strategies: problem solving, problem-oriented policing and community–oriented policing. In S. T. O'Connor and A. Grant (eds.), *Problem-oriented policing: crime-specific problems, critical issues, and making POP work*. Washington, DC: Police Executive Research Forum.

Clarke, R., and Cornish, D. (1985). Modeling offenders' decisions: a framework for research and policy. In M. Tonry and M. Norris (eds.), *Crime and justice: an annual review of research*, vol. 6. Chicago, IL: University of Chicago Press.

Clarke, R., and Eck, J. (2005). *Crime analysis for problem solvers in 60 small steps*. Washington, DC: Office of Community Oriented Policing Services, U.S. Department of Justice.

Clarke, R. V., and Mayhew, P. (eds.) (1980). *Designing out crime*. London: Home Office Research Unit, Her Majesty's Stationery Office.

Cohen, L., and Felson, M. (1979). Social change and crime rate trends: a routine activity approach. *American Sociological Review* 44:588–605.

Cohen, L., Kluegel, J., and Land, K. (1981). Social inequality and predatory criminal victimization: an exposition and test of a formal theory. *American Sociological Review* 46(5):505–24.

Comeau, M., Duda, J., Petitti, N., and Klofas, J. (2011). *Analysis of 2010 Rochester City pawn shop transactions*. Working paper 2011–03. Rochester, NY: Center for Public Safety Initiatives, Rochester Institute of Technology.

Cornish, D., and Clarke, R. (eds.) (1986). *The reasoning criminal: rational choice perspectives on offending*. New York: Springer.

Cozens, P., and Love, T. (2015). A review and current status of Crime Prevention through Environmental Design (CPTED). *Journal of Planning Literature* 30(4):1–20.

Dehejia, R., and Wahba, S. (1999). Causal effects in nonexperimental settings: reevaluating the evaluation of training programs. *Journal of the American Statistical Association* 94:1053–62.

Drawve, G. (2014). A metric comparison of predictive hot spot techniques and RTM. *Justice Quarterly* 33(3):369–97.

Drawve, G., Thomas, S. A., and Walker, J. T. (2016). Bringing the physical environment back into neighborhood research: the utility of RTM for developing an aggregate neighborhood risk of crime measure. *Journal of Criminal Justice* 44:21–29.

Dugato, M. (2013). Assessing the validity of risk terrain modeling in a European city: preventing robberies in the city of Milan. *Crime Mapping* 5:63–89.

Eck, J. (2002). Preventing crime at places. In L. Sherman, D. Farrington, B. Welsh, and D. Mackenzie (eds.), *Evidence-based crime prevention*, 241–94. New York: Routledge.

Eck, J. (1983). *Solving crimes: The investigation of burglary and robbery*. Washington, DC: Police Executive Research Forum.

Eck, J., and Spelman, W. (1987). *Problem-solving: problem-oriented policing in Newport News*. Washington, DC: Police Executive Research Forum.

Eck, J. and Weisburd, D. (eds.)(1995). *Crime and place. Crime prevention stuides, volume 4*. Monsey, NY: Criminal Justice Press.

Ericson, R., and Haggerty, K. (1997). *Policing the risk society*. Toronto: University of Toronto Press.

Eterno, J., and Silverman, E. (2012). *The crime numbers game: management by manipulation*. Boca Raton, FL: CRC Press.

Farrington, D., Gill, M., Waples, S., and Argomaniz, J. (2007). The effects of closed-circuit television on crime: meta-analysis of an English national quasi-experimental multi-site evaluation. *Journal of Experimental Criminology* 3:21–28.

Federal Bureau of Investigation. (2014). *Crime in the United States 2013*. Washington, DC: Federal Bureau of Investigation.

Ferguson, A. (2012). Predictive policing and reasonable suspicion. *Emory Law Review* 62: 259–325.

Ferguson, A. (2017). *The rise of big data policing: surveillance, race, and the future of law enforcement.* New York: NYU Press.

Ferrandino, J. (2016). The effectiveness and equity of NYPD stop and frisk policy, 2003–2014. *Journal of Crime and Justice* 41(2):119–35. doi: 10.1080/0735648X.2016.1249385.

Fogelson, R. (1977). *Big-city police.* Cambridge, MA: Harvard University Press.

Gaines, L., and Kappeler, V. (2005). *Policing in America.* 5th ed. New York: Lexis Nexus, Anderson.

Garnier, S., J. M. Caplan, and L. W. Kennedy (2018). Predicting Dynamical Crime Distribution From Environmental and Social Influences. *Frontiers of Applied Mathematics and Statistics,* 4:13.

Gibbs, J. (1986). Punishment and deterrence: theory, research, and penal policy. In L. Lipson and S. Wheeler (eds.), *Law and the social sciences.* New York: Russel Sage.

Giambusso, D. (February 1, 2012). Ordinance limiting hours of late night Newark eateries passes unanimously. *Star-Ledger.*

Goldstein, H. (1979). Improving policing : a problem-oriented approach. *Crime & Delinquency* 25(2):236–58.

Goldstein, H. (1990). *Problem-oriented policing.* New York: McGraw-Hill.

Greene, J. (2000). Community policing in America: changing the nature, structure, and function of the police. *Criminal Justice* 3(3):299–378.

Greene, J. (2014). New directions in policing: balancing predictions and meaning in police research. *Justice Quarterly* 31(2):193–228.

Greenwood, P., Chaiken, J., and Petersilia, J. (1977). *The Investigation Process.* Lexington, MA: Lexington Books.

Groff, E. R., Ratcliffe, J. H., Haberman, C. P., Sorg, E. T., Joyce, N. M., and Taylor, R. B. (2015). Does what police do at hot spots matter? The Philadelphia Policing Tactics Experiment. *Criminology* 53(1):23–53.

Guilfoyle, S. (2015). Binary comparisons and police performance measurement: good or bad? *Policing, A Journal of Policy and Practice,* 9(2): 195–209.

Gundhus, G. O. (2005). "Catching" and "targeting": risk-based policing, local culture and gendered practices. *Journal of Scandinavian Studies in Criminology and Crime Prevention* 6(2).

Haberman, C. P. (2016). A view inside the "'black box'" of hot spots policing from a sample of police commanders. *Police Quarterly* 19(4):488–517.

Hagan, J. (1989). Why is there so little criminal justice theory? Neglected macro- and micro-level links between organization and power. *Journal of Research in Crime and Delinquency* 26(2):116–35.

Hart, T. C., and Zandbergen, P. A. (2012). *Effects of data quality on predictive hotspot mapping.* Washington, DC: National Institute of Justice.

Hart, T. C., and Zandbergen, P. A. (2014). Kernel density estimation and hotspot mapping: examining the influence of interpolation method, grid cell size, and bandwidth on crime forecasting. *Policing: An International Journal of Police Strategies & Management* 37(2):305–23.

Higginson, A., and Mazerolle, L. (2014). Legitimacy policing of places: the impact on crime and disorder. *Journal of Experimental Criminology* 10: 429–57.

Huet, E. (2015, March 2). Server and protect: predictive policing firm PredPol promises to map crime before it happens. *Forbes.* Retrieved from https://www.forbes.com/sites/ellenhuet/2015/02/11/predpol-predictive-policing/.

Huey, L., and Mitchell, R. J. (2016). Unearthing hidden keys: why pracademics are an invaluable (if underutilized) resource in policing research. *Policing: A Journal of Policy and Practice* 10(3):300–07.

Jenkins, M., and DeCarlo, J. (2015). *Police leaders in the new community problem-solving era.* Durham, NC: Carolina Academic Press.

Johnson, S., Tilley, N., and Bowers, K. (2015). Introducing EMMIE: an evidence rating scale to encourage mixed-method crime prevention synthesis reviews. *Journal of Experimental Criminology* 11(3):459–73.

Jordan, June. (1970). "Corners on the Curving Sky." In J. Jordan (ed.), *Soulscript.* New York: Harlem Moon.

Kansas City, Missouri, Police Department (1977). *Response time analysis: volume II, part 1, Crime analysis.* Washington, DC: Office of Justice Programs, National Institute of Justice, United States Department of Justice.

Keay, S., and Kirby, S. (2017). The evolution of the police analyst and the influence of evidence-based policing. *Policing: A Journal of Policy & Practice.* doi: 10.1093/police/pax065.

Kelling, G., and Coles, C. (1996). *Fixing broken windows: restoring order and reducing crime in our communities.* New York: Simon and Schuster.

Kelling, G., Pate, T., Dieckman, D., and Brown, C. (1974). *The Kansas City Preventive Patrol Experiment.* Washington, DC: Police Foundation.

Kennedy, D. (1997). Pulling levers: chronic offenders, high-crime settings, and a theory of prevention. *Valparaiso University Law Review* 31:449–84.

Kennedy, L. W. (1983). *The urban kaleidoscope: Canadian perspectives.* Toronto: McGraw-Hill Ryerson.

Kennedy, L. W., Caplan, J. M., and Piza, E. (2011). Risk clusters, hotspots, and spatial intelligence: risk terrain modeling as an algorithm for police resource allocation strategies. *Journal of Quantitative Criminology* 27(3):339–62.

Kennedy, L. W., Caplan, J. M., and Piza, E. L. (2015). *A multi-jurisdictional test of risk terrain modeling and place based evaluation of environmental risk-based patrol deployment strategies.* Newark, NJ: Rutgers Center on Public Security. http://www.rutgerscps.org/uploads/2/7/3/7/27370595/nij6city_resultsexecsum_final.pdf

Kennedy, L. W., Caplan, J. M., Piza, E. L., and Buccine-Schraeder, H. (2016). Vulnerability and exposure to crime: applying risk terrain modeling to the study of assault in Chicago. *Applied Spatial Analysis and Policy* 9(4):529–48.

Kennedy, L. W., and Forde, D. R. (1998). *When push comes to shove: a routine conflict approach to violence.* Albany: State University of New York Press.

Kennedy, L. W., and Van Brunschot, E. G. (2009). *The risk in crime.* Lanham, MD: Rowman and Littlefield.

Kennedy, L. W., Irvin-Erikson, Y., and Kennedy, A. (2014). *Translational criminology and counter-terrorism: global threats and local responses.* New York: Springer.

Klofas, J., Hipple, N., and McGarrell, E. (eds.) (2010). *The new criminal justice: American communities and the changing world of crime control.* New York: Routledge.

Kondo, M., Keene, D., Hohl, B., MacDonald, J., and Branas, C. (2015). A difference-in-differences study of the effects of a new abandoned building remediation strategy on safety. *PLoS ONE* 10(7). doi: 10.1371/journal.pone.0129582.

Koss, K. (2015). Leveraging predictive policing algorithms to restore Fourth Amendment protections in high-crime areas in a post-Wardlow world. *Chicago-Kent Law Review* 90(1):301–34.

LaFree, G. (1998). *Losing legitimacy: street crime and the decline of social institutions in America.* Boulder, CO: Westview Press.

Leigh, A., Read, T., and Tilley, N. (1996). *Problem-oriented policing.* Paper 75. Crime Detection and Prevention Series. London: Police Research Group, Home Office.

Levine, N. (2004) *CrimeStat III: a spatial statistics program for the analysis of crime incident locations* (version 3.0). Houston, TX: Ned Levine & Associates. Washington, DC: National Institute of Justice.

Levine, N. (2008). The "hottest" part of a hotspot: comments on "The utility of hotspot mapping for predicting spatial patterns of crime." *Security Journal* 21:295–302.

Lewin, K. (1947). Group decision and social change. In T. Newcomb and E. Hartley (eds.), *Readings in social psychology*, 202–03. New York: Holt and Company.

Lewis, M. (2016). *The Undoing Project: a friendship that changed our minds.* New York: W. W. Norton & Company.

Lipsey, M., and Wilson, D. (2001). *Practical meta-analysis.* Applied Social Research Methods Series. Thousand Oaks, CA: Sage.

Louiselli, J. K., and Cameron, M. J. (eds.) (1998). *Antecedent control: innovative approaches to behavioral support.* Baltimore, MD: Brookes.

Lum, C., and Koper, C. (2017). *Evidence-based policing: translating research into practice.* Oxford: Oxford University Press.

Lynch, K. (1960) *The Image of the City.* Cambridge, MA: MIT Press.

MacQueen, S., and Bradford, B. (2016). Where did it all go wrong? Implementation failure—and more—in a field experiment of procedural justice policing. *Journal of Experimental Criminology* 13(3):321–45. doi: 10.1007/s11292-016-9278-7.

Maguire, E., Uchida, C., and Hassell, K. (2015). Problem-oriented policing in Colorado Springs: a content analysis of 753 cases. *Crime & Delinquency* 61:71–95.

Maguire, M. 2000. Policing by risks and targets: some dimensions and implications of intelligence-led crime control. *Policing and Society* 9(4):315–36.

Manning, P. (2008). *The technology of policing: crime mapping, information technology, and the rationality of crime control.* New York: New York University Press.

Maple, J., and Mitchell, C. (1999). *The crime fighter: how you can make your community crime-free.* New York: Broadway Books.

Marsh, M. H., & Noonan, T. E. (2005). Risk Management Approaches To Protection: Final Report And Recommendations By The Council. *National Infrastructure Advisory Council.*

Martin, P., and Mazerolle, L. (2016). Police leadership in fostering evidence-based agency reform. *Policing: A Journal of Policy and Practice* 10(1):34–43.

Mastrofski, S. (2006). Community policing: a skeptical view. In D. Weisburd and A. Braga (eds.), *Police innovation: contrasting perspectives*, 44–73. New York: Cambridge University Press.

Mastrofski, S., & Willis, J. (2011). Police organization. In M. Tonry (Ed.), *The Oxford handbook of crime and criminal justice* (pp. 479–508). Oxford: Oxford University Press.

Mazerolle, L., and Ransley, J. (2006). The case for third-party policing. In D. Weisburd and A. Braga (eds.), *Police innovation: contrasting perspectives,* 191–221. New York: Cambridge University Press.

McCollister, K., French, M. T., and Feng, H. (2010). The cost of crime to society: new crime-specific estimates for policy and program evaluation. *Drug and Alcohol Dependence* 108 (1–2):98–109.

McGloin, J, C. Sullivan, and L. Kennedy. (2011) *When Crime Appears: The Role of Emergence.* NY; Routledge.

Melamed, S. (August 10, 2017). Can Atlantic City's bold experiment take racial bias out of predictive policing? *Philadelphia Inquirer.*

Mock, L. (2010). Action research for crime control and prevention. In J. Klofas, N. Hipple, and E. McGarrell (eds.), *The new criminal justice: American communities and the changing world of crime control.* New York:Routledge.

Nagin, D., Solow, R., and Lum, C. (2015). Deterrence, criminal opportunities, and police. *Criminology* 53(1):74–100.

Nolette, J. (2015). Using research to move policing forward. *NIJ Journal* no. 276, 1–5.

Papachristos, A. (2011). Too big to fail: the science and politics of violence prevention. *Criminology & Public Policy* 10(4):1053–61.

Papachristos, A., Braga, A., Piza, E., and Grossman, L. (2015). The company you keep? The spillover effects of gang membership on individual gunshot victimization in a co-offending network. *Criminology* 53(4):624–49.

Perry, W., McInnis, B., Price, C., Smith, S., and Hollywood, J. (2013). *Predictive policing: the role of crime forecasting in law enforcement operations.* Santa Monica, CA: RAND Corporation, Safety and Justice Program.

Moreto, W., Piza, E., and Caplan, J. (2014). A Plague on Both Your Houses? Risks, Repeats, and Reconsiderations of Urban Residential Burglary. *Justice Quarterly, 31*(6): 1102–1126.

Piza, E. (forthcoming). The effect of various police enforcement actions on violent crime: evidence from a saturation foot-patrol intervention. *Criminal Justice Policy Review,* doi: 10.1177/0887403417725370.

Piza, E., Caplan, J., and Kennedy, L. (2014). Analyzing the influence of micro-level factors on CCTV camera effect. *Journal of Quantitative Criminology* 30(2):237–64.

Piza, E., Caplan, J., Kennedy, L., and Gilchrist, A. (2015). The effects of merging proactive CCTV monitoring with directed police patrol: a randomized controlled trial. *Journal of Experimental Criminology* 11(1):43–69.

Piza, E., and Feng, S. (2017). The current and potential role of crime analysts in evaluations of police interventions: results from a survey of the International Association of Crime Analysts. *Police Quarterly* 20(4):339–66.

Piza, E., and O'Hara, B. (2014). Saturation foot patrol in a high-violence area: a quasi-experimental evaluation. *Justice Quarterly* 31(4):693–718.

Pizzaro, J. and J. McGloin (2006) Explaining Gang Homicides in Newark, N.J. *Journal of Criminal Justice,* 4(2), March-April 2006, pp. 195–207.

Potchak, M., J. McGloin, and K. Zgoba (2002) A Spatial Analysis of Criminal Effort: Auto Theft in Newark, New Jersey. *Criminal Justice Policy Review,* 13(3):257–285.

Pyrooz, D., Decker, S., Wolfe, S., and Shjarback, J. (2016). Was there a Ferguson Effect on crime rates in large U.S. cities? *Journal of Criminal Justice* 46(1):1–8.

Rahr, S., and Rice, S. K. (2015). *From warriors to guardians: recommitting American police culture to democratic ideals.* Cambridge, MA: Harvard Kennedy School of Government, Program in Criminal Justice Policy and Management, Executive Session on Policing and Public Safety. Washington, DC: Office of Justice Programs, National Institute of Justice, US Department of Justice.

Ratcliffe, J., and Breen, C. (2008). Spatial Evaluation of Police Tactics in Context (SEPTIC) spreadsheet, version 3 (spring 2010). Retrieved from www.jratcliffe.net.

Read, T., and Tilley, N. (2000). Executive summary. *Not rocket science? Problem-solving and crime reduction.* Crime Reduction Research Series, paper 6. London: Policing and Reducing Crime Unit, Home Office.

Reaves, B. A. (2016). State and local law enforcement training academies, 2013. Washington, DC: Bureau of Justice Statistics Bulletin, U.S. Department of Justice.

Reboussin, R., Warren, J., and Hazelwood, R. (1995). Mapless mapping in analyzing the spatial distribution of serial rapes. In C. Block, M. Dabdoub, and S. Freegley (eds.), *Crime analysis through computer mapping,* 69–74. Washington, DC: Police Executive Research Forum.

Reichel, P. (1992). The misplaced emphasis on urbanization in police development. *Policing and Society* 3(1):1–12.

Rengert, G., and Lockwood, B. (2009). Geographical units of analysis and the analysis of crime. In D. Weisburd, W. Bernasco, and G. Bruinsma (eds.), *Putting crime in its place: units of analysis in geographic criminology.* New York: Springer.

Rengifo, A., Stemen, D., and Amidon, E. (2017). When policy comes to town: discourse and dilemmas on implementation of a statewide reentry policy in Kansas. *Criminology* 55(3):603–30. doi: 10.1111/1745-9125.12146.

Reppetto, T. (1978). *The blue parade.* New York: Free Press.

Rice, S. (May 3, 2017). What new Texas moms should know about those free baby boxes. *Dallas News.*

Rosenbaum, P., and Rubin, D. (1985). Constructing a control group using multivariate matched sampling methods that incorporate the propensity score. *American Statistician* 39(1):33–38.

Sacco, V., and Kennedy, L. W. (2002). *The criminal event: perspective in space and time.* 2nd ed. Belmont, CA: Wadsworth.

Sampson, R. J., and Raudenbush, S. W. (1999). Systematic social observation of public spaces: a new look at disorder in urban neighborhoods. *American Journal of Sociology* 105: 603–51.

Santos, R. B. (2013a). *Crime analysis with crime mapping.* Thousand Oaks, CA: Sage.

Santos, R. B. (2013b). Implementation of a police organizational model for crime reduction. *Policing: An International Journal of Police Strategies & Management* 36(2),295–311.

Santos, R. B. (2014). The effectiveness of crime analysis for crime reduction: cure or diagnosis? *Journal of Contemporary Criminal Justice* 30(2):147–68.

Santos, R. B., and Taylor, B. (2014). The integration of crime analysis into police patrol work: results from a national survey of law enforcement agencies. *Policing: An International Journal of Police Strategies & Management* 37(3):501–20.

Schnell, C., Braga, A. A., and Piza, E. L. (2016). The influence of community areas, neighborhood clusters, and street segments on the spatial variability of violent crime in Chicago. *Journal of Quantitative Criminology* 33(3):469–96. doi: 10.1007/s10940–016–9313-x.

Scott, M. (2010). Implementing crime prevention: lessons learned from problem-oriented policing projects. In J. Knutsson and R. Clarke (eds.), *Putting theory to work: implementing situational prevention and problem-oriented policing*. Crime Prevention Studies, volume 20. Boulder, CO: Lynne Rienner.

Secret, M., Abell, L., and Berline, T. (2011). The promise and challenge of practice-research collaborations: guiding principles and strategies for initiating, designing, and implementing program evaluation research. *Social Work* 56(1):9–20.

Shane, J. (2007). *What every chief executive should know: using data to measure police performance.* Flushing, NY: Looseleaf.

Sherman, L. (1998). *Evidence-based policing. Ideas in policing series.* Washington, DC: Police Foundation.

Sherman, L., and Eck, J. (2002). Policing for crime prevention. In L. Sherman, D. Farrington, B. Welsh, and D. Mackenzie (eds.), *Evidence-based crime prevention*, revised ed., 295–329. New York: Routledge.

Sherman, L., Gartin, P. R., and Buerger, M. E. (1989). Hot spots of predatory crime: routine activities and the criminology of place. *Criminology* 27(1):27–55.

Sherman, L., and Rogan, D. (1995). Effects of gun seizures on gun violence: "hot spots" patrol in Kansas City. *Justice Quarterly* 12(4): 673–93.

Sherman, L., and Weisburd, D. (1995). General deterrent effects of police patrol in crime "hot spots": a randomized, controlled trial. *Justice Quarterly* 12(4):625–48.

Shjarback, J., Pyrooz, D., Wolfe, S., and Decker, S. (2017). De-policing and crime in the wake of Ferguson: racialized changes in the quantity and quality of policing among Missouri police departments. *Journal of Criminal Justice* 50:42–52.

Silverman, E. (2006). Compstat's innovation. In D. Weisburd and A. Braga (eds.), *Police innovation: contrasting perspectives*, 267–83. New York: Cambridge University Press.

Sklansky, D. A. (2011). *The persistent pull of police professionalism.* Cambridge, MA: Harvard Kennedy School of Government, Program in Criminal Justice Policy and Management, Executive Session on Policing and Public Safety. Washington, DC: Office of Justice Programs, National Institute of Justice, US Department of Justice.

Skogan, W. G. (1990). *Disorder and decline.* New York: Free Press.

Skogan, W., and Frydl, K. (2004). *Fairness and effectivenss in policing: the evidence.* Committee to Review Research on Police Policy and Practices. Committee on Law and Justice, Divison of Behavioral and Social Sciences and Education. Washington, DC: National Academies Press.

Smith, K. (2018, January 1). We were wrong about stop-and-frisk: crime in New York City fell even as the policing tactic was abandoned. *National Review.* Retrieved from http://www.nationalreview.com/article/455035/new-york-city-stop-and-frisk-crime-decline-conservatives-wrong.

Sorg, E., Wood, J., Groff, E., and Ratcliffe, J. (2014). Boundary adherence during place-based policing evaluations: a research note. *Journal of Research in Crime and Delinquency* 51(3):377–93.

Sparrow, M. (2008). *The character of harms: operational challenges in control.* New York: Cambridge University Press.

Sparrow, M. (2011). *Governing science*. New Perspectives in Policing. Harvard University Executive Session on Policing and Public Safety. Cambridge, MA: Harvard Kennedy School of Government, Program in Criminal Justice Policy and Management, Executive Session on Policing and Public Safety. Washington, DC: Office of Justice Programs, National Institute of Justice, US Department of Justice.

Sparrow, M. (2015). Measuring performance in a modern police organization. National Institute of Justice, U.S. Department of Justice,.

Sparrow, M. (2016). *Handcuffed: what holds policing back, and the keys to reform*. Washington, DC: Brookings Institution Press.

Sparrow, M., Moore, M. H., and Kennedy, D. M. (1990). *Beyond 911: a new era for policing*. New York: Basic Books.

Spelman, W., and Brown, D. (1981). *Calling the police: citizen reporting of serious crime*. Washington, DC: Police Executive Research Forum.

Spiegel, A. (2015, January 5). What heroin addiction tells us about changing bad habits. NPR Blogs. Retrieved from http://www.npr.org/blogs/health/2015/01/05/371894919/what-heroin-addiction-tells-us-about-changing-bad-habits

Star Ledger (2010, November 30). Newark finalizes 167 police layoffs after union refuses Booker's plea to return to negotiating table. Retrieved from http://www.nj.com/news/index.ssf/2010/11/union_head_expects_167_newark.html.

Strenger, E. W. (December 21, 2016). Caplan's crime-reduction model expected to make AC a safer place. *Voice at the Shore*.

Sweeten, G. (2016). What works, what doesn't, what's constitutional? The problem with assessing an unconstitutional police practice. *Criminology and Public Policy* 15(1):67–73.

Taylor, B., Kowalyk, A., and Boba, R. (2007). The integration of crime analysis into law enforcement agencies: an exploratory study into the perceptions of crime analysts. *Police Quarterly* 10(2):154–69.

Towers, S., and White, M. (2017). The "Ferguson Effect," or too many guns? Exploring violent crime in Chicago. *Significance* (April), 26–29.

Travis, J., Western, B., and Redburn, S. (2014). *The growth of incarceration in the United States: exploring causes and consequences*. Washington, DC: National Research Council of the National Academies. National Academies Press.

U.S. Census Bureau (2015). *Quickfacts from US census bureau: Colorado Srings, CO*. Washington, DC: Census Bureau.

U.S. Census Bureau (2010). *Decennial census sumary file 1*. Washington, DC: Census Bureau.

Varon, J. (1975). A reexamination of the law enforcement assitance administration. *Stanford Law Review*, 27: 1303–1324.

Van Brunschot, E., and L. Kennedy (2008). *Risk Balance and Security*. Thousand Oaks, CA: Sage.

Visher, S., and Weisburd, D. (1998). Identifying what works: recent trends in crime prevention strategies. *Crime, Law and Social Change* 28:223–42.

Walker, S., and Katz, C. (2005). *The police in America: an introduction*. 5th ed. New York: McGraw-Hill.

Wartell, J., and Gallagher, K. (2012). Translating environmental criminology theory into crime analysis practice. *Policing: A Journal of Policy and Practice* 6(4):377–87.

Weisburd, D. (2008). *Place-based policing.* Ideas in Policing Series. Washington, DC: Police Foundation.

Weisburd, D., and Braga, A. (2006). Introduction: understanding police innovation. In D. Wesiburd and A. Braga (eds.), *Police innovation: contrasting perspectives.* Cambridge: Cambridge University Press.

Weisburd, D., Bushway, S. D., Lum, C. M., and Yang, S. M. (2004). Trajectories of crime at places: a longitudinal study of street segments in the city of Seattle. *Criminology* 42(2): 283–321.

Weisburd, D., and Eck, J. (2004). What can police do to reduce crime, disorder, and fear? *Annals of the American Academy of Political and Social Science* 593(1):42–65.

Weisburd, D., and Green, L. (1995). Policing drug hot spots: the Jersey City Drug Market Analysis Experiment. *Justice Quarterly* 12(4):711–36.

Weisburd, D., Mastrofski, S. D., McNally, A. M., Greenspan, R., and Willis, J. J. (2003). Reforming to preserve: CompStat and strategic problem solving in American policing. *Criminology & Public Policy* 2(3):421–56.

Weisburd, D., Telep, C. W., Hinkle, J. C., and Eck, J. E. (2010). Is problem-oriented policing effective in reducing crime and disorder? *Criminology & Public Policy* 9(1),139–72.

Wellford, C. (2009). Criminologists should stop whining about their impact on policy and practice. In N. A. Frost, J. D. Freilich, and T. R. Clear (eds.), *Contemporary issues in criminal justice policy* (1st ed.), 17–24. Belmont, CA: Wadsworth Cengage.

Welsh, B., and Farrington, D. (2009a). Public area CCTV and crime prevention: an updated systematic review and meta-analysis. *Justice Quarterly* 26(4):716–45.

Welsh, B., and Farrington, D. (2009b). *Making public places safer: surveillance and crime prevention.* New York: Oxford University Press.

Welsh, W., and Harris, P. (2016). *Criminal justice policy and planning.* 5th ed. New York: Routledge.

Wheeler, A. P., Mclean, S. J., and Worden, R. E. (2016). Replicating group-based trajectory models of crime at micro-places in Albany, NY. *Journal of Quantitative Criminology* 32(4):589–612.

Willis, J., Mastrofski, S., and Weisburd, D. (2007). Making sense of COMPSTAT: a theory-based analysis of organizational change in three police departments. *Law & Society Review* 41(1):147–88.

Wilson, J. Q., and Kelling, G. L. (1982). Broken windows: the police and neighborhood safety. *Atlantic Monthly* (March), 29–38.

Wilson, O. W. (1963). *Police administration.* New York: McGraw-Hill.

Wortley, R., and Mazerolle, L. (2008). Environmental criminology and crime analysis: situating the theory, analytic approach and application. In R. Wortley and L. Mazerolle (eds.), *Environmental criminology and crime analysis,* 1–15. Portland, OR: Willian.

Wright, R., and Decker, S. (1994). *Burglars on the job.* Boston, MA: Northeastern University Press.

Wu, X., and Lum, C. (2016). Measuring the spatial and temporal patterns of police proactivity. *Journal of Quantitative Criminology* 33(4):915–34. doi: 10.1007/s10940-016-9318-5.

INDEX

Abell, L. 103
ACTION (Assessments, Connections, Tasks, Interventions, Outcomes, and Notifications) 36–39, 42, 44, 46, 53, 61, 109, 120, 124, 125, 133
    ACTION meetings vi, vii, 35–37, 39, 41, 46, 47, 109, 110, 117–119, 121, 123, 131, 132, 134, 136
aggregate neighborhood risk of crime (ANROC) 53, 60–62
Agnew, R. 20
Amidon, E. 105
Anderson, G. 73
Andresen, M. 55
Apel, R. 74
Ariel, B. 108, 109
Atlantic City, NJ vii, 27, 31, 42, 118–125, 129
Austin, P. 73
average treatment effect on the treated (ATT) 74, 75, 79, 80table, 85, 90, 91table, 96, 97table

Barnum, J. D. 55, 65
Beck, U. 36

behavior settings 8, 9, 23, 24, 30, 53, 129, 130
behavior patterns 25, 55
Berline, T. 103
Berman, G. 105
Bernasco, W. 12
Blackburn, B. 32
Block, C. R. 64
Block, R. 12, 64
Boba, R. 115
Bond, B. J. 19
Bowers, K. 104, 111, 112, 116
Bradford, B. 106
Braga, A. 15–20, 55, 78, 81, 89, 103
Brantingham, P. J. 18, 54, 56, 57
Brantingham, P. L. 18, 54, 56, 57
Bratton, W. 5, 19
Brooklyn, NY 65, 66, 67, 68, 105
Brown, D. 16
Brown, R. 108
Buerger, M. 17, 20, 103
Burgess, E. W. 58
Bursik, R. 60

Cameron, M. J. 55

Caplan, J. M. ix, xii, 12, 18, 22, 24, 33, 34, 54, 62, 64, 66, 68, 72, 87, 101, 104, 107, 108, 116, 134
catchment zones 79, 80table, 89, 90, 91table, 96, 97table
Chainey, S. 64, 65
Cissner, A. 104, 105
Clarke, R. V. 17, 18, 19, 54, 55
Cohen, L. 18, 20, 54, 55
Coles, C. 15, 16, 104
Colorado Springs, CO vi, 71, 73, 76, 77, 78fig, 79fig, 99table, 105, 112, 118
Comeau, M. 116
community engagement 5, 7, 32, 36, 84, 86, 106, 108
    community policing 17, 19, 37
Cornish, D. 18, 54, 55
Cozens, P. 58
crime analysis ix, 8, 9, 12, 13, 17, 18, 21, 25, 26, 31, 39, 53, 68, 109, 111, 115, 126, 127, 134
crime attractors 12, 23, 30, 35, 36, 55, 56, 59, 125, 129, 130
crime displacement 25, 42
crime generators 55, 56, 109, 127
crime patterns 9, 18, 33, 54, 55, 56, 64
crime prevention 3, 5–8, 10–12, 14, 16, 17, 18, 20–23, 26, 30–33, 36, 41, 46, 47, 54, 56, 58, 59, 65, 70, 100, 102, 108, 118, 120, 127, 130, 135
crime prevention through environmental design (CPTED) 54, 58, 95
crime problems ix, 5, 7–9, 17–20, 24, 25, 28, 29, 31, 33, 35, 36, 40, 46, 59, 70, 87, 100, 119, 121, 124, 130, 131
crime risk 3, 29, 37, 43, 44, 54, 60, 61, 62, 110, 128, 131
crime risk kaleidoscope 53, 57, 62, 130, 134
criminal behavior ix, 6–9, 24, 26, 31, 56, 128, 129

data-driven (decisions/approaches) vi, 19, 27, 30, 36, 44, 45, 46, 121, 124, 126–128, 132, 133, 135
DeCarlo, J. 13
decision-making 3, 25, 33, 35, 39, 41, 43, 44, 45, 46, 120, 126, 127, 128
Decker, S. 116
Dehejia, R. 73

Drawve, G. 60, 64, 65, 66, 68, 120
Dugato, M. 65

Eck, J. 16–18, 55, 92, 104
environmental attractors ix, 64, 71, 128, 129, 130
environmental backcloth 57, 58
environmental contexts 24, 55, 130
environmental criminology 18, 24, 54, 55, 58
environmental risk 9, 30, 59, 66, 122
Ericson R. ix
Eterno, J. 19
evidence-based ix, xi, 3, 5, 8, 10, 11, 17, 18, 21, 28, 31, 33, 35, 41, 43, 62, 70, 92, 103, 115, 116, 124, 128, 131, 133, 134

Farole, D. 104, 105
Felson, M. 18, 20, 54, 55
Feng, H. 42
Feng, S. 31, 115
Ferguson, A. 8, 26, 124
Ferrandino, J. 28
Fogelson, R. 14
Forde, D. R. 55
Fox, A. 105
French, M. T. 42
Frydl, K. 12, 16–18,

Gaines, L. 13, 14
Gallagher, K. 18
Gartin, P. R. 17, 20
geographic modus operandi 123
Giambusso, D. 44
Glendale, AZ vi, 71, 74, 81, 82fig, 83, 84fig, 99fig
Goldstein, H. 17, 104
Green, L. 78, 89
Greene, J. 13, 99
Greenwood, P. 16
Groff, E. R. 18
Grootendorst, P. 73
Guilfoyle, S. 19
Gundhus, G. O. ix

Haberman, C. P. 12
Hagan, J. 104, 116
Haggerty, K. ix
Harris, P. 72, 104, 105, 107, 116, 117

Hart, T. C. 64, 66
Hazelwood, R. 20
high-risk places 30, 32, 37, 40–42, 63, 66, 68, 70–72, 80, 81, 92, 98, 100, 107, 122, 123, 129–131
Hipple, N. 15, 16, 104, 116
hot spots 7, 9, 12, 17, 18, 20–25, 28, 29, 32, 33, 41, 54, 63–66, 68–70, 120, 123, 124, 130
    hot spots policing 7, 17, 20, 21, 24, 87, 103, 130
Huet, E. 21
Hureau, D. 19, 20, 55

International Association of Crime Analysts (IACA) xi, 43
intervention x, 3, 9, 12, 17, 21, 28, 29, 31, 33, 37, 38fig, 39–42, 55, 58, 59, 61–64, 71–75, 77–80, 82–87, 89–92, 94–96, 98–105, 107, 109, 110–115, 118, 121, 125, 129, 132, 133, 135
    disaggregate intervention 75, 80, 85, 96
    during-intervention 85, 89, 96, 100
    post-intervention 42, 75, 79–81, 83, 85, 86, 89, 90–92, 95–98
    pre-intervention 73–76, 100, 111
IPIR (Intervention Planning Intel Report) 40, 119
Irvin-Erikson, Y. 62

Jenkins, M. 13
Jersey City, NJ vii, 29, 64, 118, 119, 124
Johnson, S. 104, 111, 112, 116
joint utility 64

Kansas City, MO vi, 16, 71, 76, 92, 93fig, 94, 95fig, 98, 99table, 106, 118
Kappeler, V. 13, 14
Katz, C. 13, 14
Keay, S. 115
Kelling, G. 5, 15, 16, 17, 59, 92, 104
Kennedy, D. 17, 104
Kennedy, L. W. ix, xi, 12–15, 17, 18, 21, 22, 24, 33, 34, 36, 44, 54, 55, 57, 62, 64, 66, 68, 70, 72, 87, 98, 104, 107, 108, 116
kernel density estimation (KDE) 54, 64–66, 68, 70
Kirby, S. 115
Klofas, J. 15, 16, 104, 116
Kluegel, J. 55

Knobler, P. 19
Kondo, M. 81
Koper, C. 115
Koss, K. 26, 124
Kowalyk, A. 115

LaFree, G 16
Land, K. 55
law enforcement ix, 7, 8, 9, 11, 12, 13, 15, 16, 19, 21, 23, 24, 27, 28, 30, 31, 32, 33, 36, 37, 42, 43, 48, 81, 83, 98, 115, 118, 120, 127, 132
Leigh, A. 103
Levine, N. 64
Lewin, K. 103
Lewis, M. 43–45
Little Rock, AK 60
Lockwood, B. 20
Louiselli, J. K. 55
Love, T. 58
Lum, C. 17, 108, 115
Lynch, K. 57

Maguire M. ix
Manning, P. 21
Maple, J. 19
Marsh, M. H. 46
Martin, P. 36
Mastrofski, S. 19, 103, 106, 116
Mayhew, P. 17
Mazerolle, L. 17, 36, 54, 92, 100, 101
McCollister, K. 42
McGarrell, E. ix, 15, 16, 104, 116
McGloin, J. C. 87
Mclean, S. J. 20
McQueen, S. 106
Melamed, S. 31, 32
micro-level 25, 26, 58, 60, 74, 80, 81, 85, 86, 96, 98
Miller, J. 12, 108
Mitchell, C. 19
Mitchell, R. J. 30–31
mitigate (risk) 7, 20, 23, 25, 26, 34, 36, 40, 41, 44–46, 59, 61, 71, 72, 83, 94, 98, 112, 118, 119, 124, 128, 129, 131
Mock, L. 103
Moore, M. H. 13, 14
Moreto, W. 87, 116

Nagin, D. 108
neighborhood-disorganization 60
New York City 12–14, 19, 28, 59, 65, 66
Newark, NJ vi, 15, 44, 71, 75, 87, 88, 89, 90, 92, 99, 106, 118, 134
Nolette, J. 31, 43
Noonan, T. E. 46

O'Hara, B. 87
Papachristos, A. 19, 20, 22, 55, 87, 103

Park, R. 58
Partridge, H 109
perceptions (public) 6, 8, 25, 44, 45, 56, 122
Perry, W. 21
physical decay 54, 60
physical environment 20, 53, 55, 56, 61, 131
Piza, E. xii, 12, 18, 20, 24, 31, 64, 66, 68, 72, 87, 101, 107, 109, 115, 116
Pizzaro, J. 87
place-based 11, 18–22, 26, 54, 61, 62, 64, 118, 124, 128, 131, 132
    place-based intervention 11, 20
police strategies 11, 12, 17, 19, 20, 22, 98, 107
police—community relations 32, 59, 124, 127
policing 10–22, 26–33, 36, 41, 43, 46, 47, 53, 56, 59, 62, 81, 82, 87, 92, 99, 100, 103–106, 108, 110, 111, 115, 116, 120, 121, 123, 124, 128, 130–135
    policing intervention 20, 28, 41, 55, 72, 78, 89, 110, 134
Potchak, M. C. 87
pracademics 30
prediction accuracy index (PAI) 65, 66, 68, 70
predictive validity 24, 121, 122
problem areas 12, 25, 59
problem-oriented policing 17, 19, 24, 33, 77, 82, 104
problem-solving v, 3, 7, 10, 16, 19, 23, 26, 28, 35, 43, 55, 99
Project Safe Neighborhoods 64, 103, 119
propensity score matching (PSM) 72, 73, 79, 85, 90, 96
public safety ix, xi, 7, 9, 10, 12, 15, 18, 25, 27–29, 32, 33, 35–37, 43–46, 62, 102, 103, 120, 124, 126, 127, 130, 131, 132, 133
Pyrooz, D. 28

Rahr, S. K. 16
Ransley, J. 92
Raudenbush, S. W. 60
Read, T. 19, 103
Reaves, B. A. 127
Reboussin, R. 20
Redburn, S. 16
Reichel, P. 13, 14
relative risk score (RRS) 66, 78, 82, 88, 93
relative risk value (RRV) 42, 54, 72, 77, 83, 88, 89, 94, 122, 123, 129
Rengert, G. 20
Rengifo, A. 105
Reppetto, T. 14
research-practitioner partnership vi, 31, 100, 102, 103, 106, 108, 111, 115
resource allocation 35, 36, 40, 44, 120, 134
Rice, S. 32
Rice, S. K. 16
risk assessment ix, 6, 9, 36, 37, 39, 40, 42, 44–47, 56, 60, 72, 98, 119, 123, 124, 135
risk factor 24, 25, 29, 30, 37, 39, 40–42, 53, 58, 60, 66, 67, 72, 77, 82, 83, 88, 89, 93, 94, 100, 108–110, 112, 113, 116, 118, 119, 122, 123, 129
risk governance ix, 7, 9, 28, 30–33, 35–37, 39, 40, 43, 46, 47, 53, 61, 100, 120, 125, 131, 133
risk narrative vi, 5, 9, 23, 26–30, 32, 38fig, 39, 40, 41, 43, 44, 110, 125, 128, 129, 131, 132
risk perceptions 7
risk reduction ix, 5, 7–9, 11, 24, 27, 30, 31, 34, 36, 37, 38fig, 41, 42, 46, 47, 58, 63, 64, 70, 71, 85, 100, 105, 106, 118–120, 123, 125, 127–133
risk terrain map 25, 32, 59, 66, 72, 78fig, 82fig, 88fig, 93fig, 122, 129
risk terrain model 6, 28–30, 41, 42, 47, 66–68, 72, 77, 82, 83, 88, 91, 93, 94, 100, 119, 121, 123, 128, 129
risk terrain modeling (RTM) ix, 7, 9, 21–31, 35–37, 39–43, 46, 47, 51–54, 58–61, 63–72, 77, 79, 82–84, 86, 89, 100, 128, 132–135
risk-based intervention 41, 77, 79, 81, 83, 89, 94, 99, 100, 109, 112, 113, 116, 130
risk-based policing ix-xi, 3, 5, 6–10, 21–47, 51, 53–62, 63–72, 82, 88, 93, 100, 102–104, 106, 107, 113–117, 118–128, 130–132, 134–136

risky features 23, 34, 42, 123, 129
risky places 3, 9, 18, 26, 35–37, 43, 47, 53, 54, 62–65, 70, 99, 121, 130, 131
Rogan, D. 93
Rosenbaum, P. 73
RTMDx (software) 47, 67, 68, 72, 82, 121, 128
Rubin, D. 73
Rutgers Center on Public Security xi, 72
Rutgers University xi, 13, 72, 120, 129

Sacco, V. 54
Sampson, R. J. 60
Santos, R. B. 18, 65, 111, 115
Schnell, C. 20, 81
Secret, M. 103
Sherman, L. 16, 17, 20, 93, 108
Shjarback, J. 28
Silverman, E. 19
situational contexts 27, 45, 60, 130, 131
Sklansky, D. A. 21
Skogan, W. 12, 16, 17
Smith, K. 28
social disorganization 54, 60, 61
social factors 21, 53, 60
socioeconomic-disadvantage 60
Solow, R. 108
Sorg, E. 113
Sparrow, M. 13, 14, 18, 19, 21, 31, 42, 98, 103, 106, 115, 125
spatial influence 7, 9, 24, 30, 33, 34, 39, 41, 42, 54, 58, 68, 72, 77, 82, 83, 88, 89, 93, 94, 109, 110, 112, 118, 122–124, 129, 134
spatial intelligence 12, 26, 38fig, 59
spatial risk vi, 3, 24, 25, 27, 41, 47, 60, 98, 116, 119, 122, 123, 128, 132
Spelman, W. 16, 104
Spiegel, A. 55
Stemen, D. 105
Strenger, E. W. 31
Sweeten, G 12, 74

target areas vi, 9, 26, 40, 41, 63, 64, 65, 68, 70, 72, 83, 86, 98, 113, 122, 123, 129, 131
Taylor, B. 115

Thomas, S. A. 60
Thompson, L. 64, 65
threats (security/public safety) 7, 25, 29, 32, 36, 39, 40, 41, 43–46, 120, 121, 124, 131
Tilley, N. 19, 103, 104, 116
Towers, S. 28
transparency 3, 7, 26, 32, 33, 40, 42, 46, 127, 131
Travis, J. 16

Uhlig, S. 64, 65

Van Brunschot, E. G. ix, 36, 44
Varon, J. 16
Visher, S. 103
vulnerability 6, 8, 23, 33, 43, 47, 53, 54, 61, 63–65, 68, 70
vulnerability-exposure framework 54, 63, 64, 68

Wahba, S. 73
Walker, J. T. 60
Walker, S. 13, 14
Warren, J. 20
Wartell, J. 18
Weinborn, C. 108
Weisburd, D. 15–20, 78, 89, 103, 104, 106
Wellford, C. 103
Welsh, B. 81
Welsh, W. 72, 104, 105, 107, 116, 117
Western, B. 16
Wheeler, A. P. 20
White, M. 28
Willis, J. 106, 116
Wilson, D. 101
Wilson, J. Q. 17, 59
Wilson, O. W. 14
Worden. R. E. 20
Wortley, R. 54
Wright, R. 116
Wu, X. 17

Zandbergen, P. A. 64, 66
Zgoba, K. M. 87